PRODUCT
ENTREPRENEUR

How to Launch Your Product Idea:
Napkin Sketch to $1 Million in Sales

Chris Clearman

ISBN: 978-0-578-90648-5 (Paperback)

Cover Design: Jaime Caso

For more information visit: www.ProductEntrepreneurBook.com

TABLE OF CONTENTS

PREFACE

"It is not the critic who counts;
not the man who points out how the strong man stumbles,
or where the doer of deeds could have done them better.
The credit belongs to the man who is actually in the arena,
whose face is marred by dust and sweat and blood;
who strives valiantly, who errs, who comes short again and again,
because there is no effort without error and shortcoming;
but who does actually strive to do the deeds,
who knows great enthusiasms, the great devotions;
who spends himself in a worthy cause;
who at the best knows in the end the triumph of high achievement,
and who at the worst, if he fails, at least fails while daring greatly,
so that his place shall never be with those cold and timid souls
who neither know victory nor defeat."

-Theodore Roosevelt

I've known many successful product entrepreneurs and, on average, they're no different from anyone else. It's really just the doing that sets apart the dreamers and the doers. Successful product entrepreneurs tirelessly pursue the next meaningful step forward, and they never give up. For them, there is no quitting and no defeat - only success or the opportunity to start over and try again.

Adopt this mindset and you can achieve your entrepreneurial goals.

INTRODUCTION

I hope you're adequately inspired by the preface, because that's the first and last inspirational sentiment you'll get in this book. You should prepare yourself for 14 chapters of real-world, practical information to take your product idea from a napkin sketch to your first million dollars in sales. This is the information I would have killed for when I was starting out, and much of it can't be found elsewhere. If you're just looking for an entertaining read, this probably isn't the book for you. If you're serious about turning your product idea into a thriving business, grab a pen and paper to take some notes and read on!

This book is not academic. It's written entirely from first-hand experience earned the hard way – by doing and making mistakes. I started my career as a product designer, first working for two well-known, established product companies. I launched my first product by moonlight, working on it every night after I got home from my full-time job. After moonlighting for another year-and-a-half to grow that product into a successful brand, I was able to leave my day job to pursue my dream of building my own product company. To date, my team and I operate a handful of successful product brands that we built from the ground up. We've introduced more than 40 discreet, innovative products within these brands, and I currently have over 25 patents in my name. Bringing new product ideas to market has been my obsession throughout my entire adult life. This book is the culmination of everything I've learned along the way, neatly condensed for your benefit.

The information in this book starts off pretty broad and gets vastly more detailed as we go along. Concepts introduced early in the book are built on in later chapters. In Chapter 1 we talk through some basics and building blocks to get you started. This information is critical to understanding many of the concepts we'll cover throughout the rest of the book. In Chapter 2, you'll learn how to evaluate the business potential of your ideas. Not every idea is a winner, and I'll teach you how to avoid those that most certainly aren't. Chapter 3 covers branding. Believe it or not, you need to define your target customer before you even start to design your product. Chapter 4 details the process of registering your business and setting up the basic tools you'll need to run a successful product company. Chapter 5 covers financing. You need a plan to finance your business, even if you intend to start small and use your own savings. Chapter 6 is all about accounting and taxes. This isn't anyone's favorite chapter but it's absolutely critical to your future business. In Chapter 7 we finally get to the fun part – bringing your product to life. This chapter covers design, engineering, sourcing, and manufacturing. Chapter 8 dives into logistics, teaching you how to efficiently move your product around the globe and into the hands of your customers. Chapter 9 covers the details of building your ecommerce website, and Chapter 10 teaches you how to drive traffic and sales to your site through marketing. The chapter on marketing is, by far, the longest chapter in this book. Product entrepreneurs notoriously underestimate the importance and complexity of marketing, so we really dig into the details on this subject. Chapter 11 will teach you how to turn web traffic into sales. It also covers the topic of third-party marketplaces like Amazon.com. In Chapter 12 you'll learn how to properly pitch your product to retailers and manage retail channels so you can land your brand on store shelves. Chapter 13 discusses the details and logistics of growing your company and hiring a team to help you. In chapter 14 we sum things up and outline a general order-of-operations to get you started. There is also a glossary that contains all the industry terms and acronyms that you'll need to know along the way. Check out the Table of Contents for a more detailed outline of the topics we'll cover throughout this book.

The steps and concepts covered in this book aren't strictly chronological. I tried to put the steps in order whenever possible, but it made more sense to cover topics in a sequence that built on itself. This way, a novice entrepreneur can progressively build the knowledge base necessary to understand concepts as they are presented. Chapter 14 contains a chronological summary that you can reference once you start the process of building your product business.

Throughout this book I recommend a lot of products, services, software, and other books. Every one of these recommendations is genuine. I did not receive any form of compensation from any product, service, software company, agency, or publication mentioned in this book.

They say the first million is the hardest, so I designed this book to get you there quickly and efficiently. I recommend reading this book from front to back before you start working on your product business. That will give you a great overview of the process and the project you're about to undertake. Once you get started, come back to this book frequently as a reference along the way. The information contained here can literally save you millions of dollars and thousands of hours in mistakes, research, and lost opportunity. I hope you find this compiled knowledge to be as useful as I have over the years.

CHAPTER 1:

SOME BASICS AND BUILDING BLOCKS

Before we really dive in, we need to cover a few key terms and concepts that will come up throughout the book. Commit these to memory because you'll use them daily once your business is off the ground.

Let's start with "inventory." Inventory is the stock your business holds with the goal of resale. This includes finished goods in the warehouse but may also include raw materials or individual nuts and bolts if your product hasn't been fully manufactured yet. Inventory does not include the chairs you sit on in your office or the sticky notes in your office supply drawer.

The inventory value of your finished product should include everything necessary to make your product ready for sale, all the way down to the packaging and polybags. This doesn't just include the physical components. It also includes production labor, import duties, and freight to your warehouse. This all-inclusive cost for a single unit of your product is called your "COGS" which stands for Cost of Goods Sold. "COGS" is an acronym that you'll use constantly in your product business, but you'll also hear it used interchangeably with "cost." "Cost" is the amount you pay for a given item. "Price," on the other hand, is the amount your customers pay you for the item. When you bring a product to market, you typically get to set the initial price for the end consumer. This price is called the "MSRP" which stands for Manufacturer's Suggested Retail Price.

At this point, you've probably deduced that the difference between your price and your cost is your "gross profit." Gross profit is how much money you make before any other expenses are included in the calculation. These other expenses could be staff salaries, advertising expenses, office rent, etc. The money you have left over after all expenses is your "net profit" and this is how much you take home. You'll often hear "net profit" referred to as "the bottom line" because it is literally the bottom-most line on a business's profit and loss statement.

The ratio between your price (what your customers pay) and your cost (what you pay) is very important. This relationship can be expressed as either "margin" or "markup." These are often used interchangeably but they're very different. Margin = (price-cost)/price. Markup = (price-cost)/cost. Here's an example to demonstrate the difference between these two calculations: Ex. Your cost on an item is $10 and your sell it for a price of $40. Plug these numbers into the equations above and you'll see that you have a 75% margin and a 400% markup. While these essentially mean the same thing, the numerical difference is significant and you can run into trouble if you accidentally mix these two up in a pricing negotiation. Most product-based companies use "margin" as their key metric instead of "markup."

Pro tip: If you know your cost and want to calculate your selling price with a specific margin (X), you can use the following equation to forward-calculate the margin: cost/ (1-X) : Example: Your cost is $20 and you want to know what your price should be if you take a 60% margin: $20/(1 - .60) = $50. This means you need to price your product at $50 to have a 60% margin when your cost is $20.

It's very important that you price your products so that you have ample margins. I hear so many aspiring entrepreneurs who plan to make something for $50 (COGS) and sell it to the end customer for $60 (MSRP). Their logic is always the same: "I'll make $10 every time I sell one. It'll be great!" But they're only working with a 16.7% gross margin ($60-$50)/$60=16.67%. Successful product businesses aren't built on 16% gross margins when selling directly to the end customer. Why not? Several reasons: Most obviously, you won't be able to cover your expenses with a 16% gross margin, at least not at any reasonable scale. Doing business is expensive. You have to pay for staff salaries, taxes, rent, software, office supplies, web hosting, warehouse space, insurance, utilities, and hundreds of other expenses. Second, the return on investment isn't worthwhile if you do manage to turn a meager net profit. If you're going to tie your money up investing in inventory, you need to ensure you're making a worthwhile return. As a benchmark, the S&P Index has historically returned 10% annual gains. If you're not getting a significantly better return on your investment than what a passive investment in the S&P Index would produce, save yourself the work of starting a business and just invest in an S&P ETF instead. The next issue with this low-margin logic is that you have virtually no money in your equation to acquire customers. Buying web traffic and acquiring customers is expensive. In the world of digital advertising, it's not unusual to spend $35 or more to make a $100 sale. You just can't afford to advertise your product and grow your customer base with tiny margins. Last and most importantly, distribution chains in the product business can get long and costly. There may be 3 or more middlemen between the factory and the end customer. Everyone in the chain provides some value and they all take their cut in exchange. Pricing your product incorrectly excludes the possibility of using a longer distribution chain, which can be invaluable in reaching customers and growing your product business quickly.

Before we move on, we need to talk more about distribution chains. You can't evaluate the potential of your product idea without considering what the MSRP will ultimately be, and whether customers will be willing to pay that price. To calculate a prospective MSRP, you first need to have a solid understanding of product distribution chains. We'll also take this opportunity to clearly define some terms that will be used throughout the book to ensure that we're always on the same page.

Let's start with you. You have a product idea, but you probably don't own a factory. I am going to refer to you as the "brand." Your job as the brand is to design and develop compelling products, get them manufactured, then get them into the hands of customers at a profit. You are swamped with a variety of tasks including product development, sourcing manufacturers, importing, warehousing, marketing, distributing, generating content...being a brand is no small job.

Most brands don't actually own and operate their own factories. This is typically done by a contract manufacturer who makes product for several brands. Throughout this book we will refer to the party who is physically producing the product as the "factory."

So you haven't even started your business yet and your distribution chain already contains a middle man – you! In the current example the goods are produced by the factory, sold to you, then sold by you to the end customer. That's not so bad...yet.

Pretty soon you'll start to realize that it's really difficult to get your product in front of the right customer at the right time to make the sale. This is where retail stores come into play. Throughout this book we will refer to retail stores as "retailers," "stores," or even "wholesale accounts" depending on the context. I'm sure you're already familiar with a number of retailers like Wal-Mart, Best Buy, and REI. Stores have hundreds of customers walking through their doors every day ready to spend money on products that will solve their problems. This sounds like a pretty ideal environment to place your product, right? It is! But, like everything in this industry, it's challenging and expensive to get placement in retail stores. We'll go into significant depth on getting retail placement in Chapter 12, but for now you just need to know that retailers will usually expect a minimum of 50% margin in exchange for carrying your product. This means you need to sell them your item for half of the MSRP or less! This pricing structure is known as "keystone" pricing which, oddly enough, refers to the large keystone placed in the center of a stone arch to provide stability. Just like the keystone divides the majestic stone arch in half, the retailers will expect to buy your product for half price…or something. I really don't understand the naming logic but I also don't make the rules.

While it's not the only option, the situation outlined above is a pretty common distribution chain for a product company. Let's plug some numbers in and walk through an example. Ex. The product starts at the factory. They are willing to sell you the completed product for $10. As the brand, I recommend you target 50% margins or higher when selling through this traditional distribution chain. (Your margins will be eroded from there by rep commissions, advertising allowance fees, return allowances, etc. More on that later.) Your 50% margin means you're willing to sell your product to the retail store for $20. The retail store also demands "keystone" margins which means they need to sell the product for $40 if they buy from you for $20. As it stands now, a product you can buy for $10 should have an MSRP of $40. That seems incredibly high to most newcomers, but it's actually still not high enough!

Depending on your capabilities and the retailers you want to work with, you may need to involve a distributor. "Distributors" act as middlemen between the brand and the retail stores. They already have accounts set up with the various retailers and they sell them a wide variety of products from a number of different brands. Distributors can save retail stores a considerable amount of work by enabling them to buy many of the products they stock from a single source and receive the orders in a single shipment. Distributors take care of all the shipping and logistics and they typically have software solutions called EDI (Electronic Data Interchange) that integrate with the retailers' software to automate shipping and billing. For all these reasons, retailers like working with distributors and it can often be much faster and easier to get your product placed in stores if you choose to partner with a distributor. As always, this service comes at a cost. Distributor margins are product and industry specific, but I tend to use 30% as a benchmark for distributor margins.

Let's look back at that distribution chain now. We previously had you buying from the factory for $10 and selling to the retail stores for $20. Now we've decided to interject a distributor who wants 30% margins between you and the store. This means you're selling to the distributor for $20, they're selling to the store for $28.57, and the store is selling to the end customer for $57.14! With this distribution chain, the item that costs you $10 has an MSRP of nearly $60!

There are a few other things to consider. One of the most important is that this equation assumes there is no cost in getting the product from the factory to your warehouse. This couldn't be more wrong, especially if you're manufacturing in a foreign country. Shipping product from around the world is relatively expensive and import duties can cost an arm and a leg. Ocean freight cost varies greatly based on the density of your product but I usually like to add in 10% of the item cost for shipping as a preliminary placeholder. Also, import duties (AKA tariffs) on consumer products tend to range from 5%-20% (as of this writing in 2021 punitive duties on products imported to the U.S. from China are commonly near 50%) and they're different for each product category. We'll go into detail on freight and duties in Chapter 8, but for now you need to know that you should expect a significant expense in shipping and importing your product, and that should be included in your pricing calculation.

One opposing factor that can help to lower MSRP in long distribution chains is that each party in the chain will often accept slightly lower margins since the work is divided amongst the longer supply chain. If you decide to use a distributor to help you break into retail stores, you likely won't need to employ a sales team or exhibit independently at expensive industry trade shows. Your distributor should do these things for you. As such, you can accept a lower margin because you have lower expenses. On the other end of the equation, working with a distributor can provide a lot of convenience and efficiency for retail stores, so they are often willing to accept slightly lower margins.

Let's go through the calculation again with all of these considerations in place and assume you're using a factory in SE Asia: You buy the product from the factory for $10. You spend an additional $1 on ocean freight (10% placeholder) and import duties on your product are 17.6% (a common duty rate on many consumer goods). Since the cost of freight is included in duty calculations, you end up with COGS at $12.94 (17.6% of $11 = $1.94 : $11 + $1.94 = $12.94). You accept a compressed margin of 40% because you plan to sell to a distributor. This puts your sale price to the distributor at $21.57. The distributor takes their 30% margin and sells to the retailer for $30.81. The retail store then adds in their compressed 40% margin and sells to the end customer for $51.35.

Let's now consider the same transaction but without the convenience of adding a distributor, and the accompanying compressed margins for brand and retailers: You buy from the factory for $10 and have an imported cost of $12.94 (refer to the math above if you already forgot how to calculate freight and duties). You have a full sales team to employ so you need your generous 50% margins, meaning you sell to the retail store for $25.88. The retailer only buys one or two items from you and there is no convenience or efficiency in dealing with you directly, so they also want a full 50% margin. This leaves the final price at $51.76.

As you can see in both examples, a product that costs you $10 from the factory should typically be sold to the end consumer for around $50 or more. For this exact reason, I recommend using a 500% markup (markup, not margin) as your minimum when evaluating your product ideas. If it costs $20 for you to buy from the factory, you should plan on setting the MSRP at $100 or more. This is much, much higher than most new entrepreneurs plan to price their products, but you need this margin structure to effectively grow a product company. You should use this 500% markup as your baseline when evaluating various product ideas. If you see the opportunity to have even larger margins, take it! A little extra margin comes in very handy once you start marketing your product.

As with every rule, there are always exceptions. You can remove middlemen from your distribution chain and lower the MSRP to offer a better value to the end consumer, but this doesn't come without challenges of its own. If you go this route you're basically betting that you can make the price of your product so attractive that customers will seek you out and flock to your product. If it works, you won't need to spend much on advertising or give retailers and distributors their cut to get your products in front of potential customers. If it doesn't work, you're left with very few options because you don't have adequate margins to operate within a more traditional distribution network. This type of business model is often referred to as "direct to consumer" or "business to consumer" which get abbreviated to "D2C" and "B2C" respectively. This style of business has become very popular with the rise of internet commerce. Through the power of the internet, brands or even foreign factories can access the consumer directly without the need for retail stores. This has proven to be a powerful avenue for many product companies and may be worth considering for your business. Another option that has really gained traction over the last decade involves brands and factories selling nearly direct to the consumer on a third party platform like Amazon. com®. Amazon® takes a significant commission, but it's still typically less than a traditional retailer. At the same time, the brand or factory can manage the product listing, advertise, manage inventory, and generally run their business entirely on the Amazon platform. Both of these strategies are viable options for launching and running a product business, but they often max out at a smaller scale than a product that is successfully channeled through a traditional distribution network. On the upside, they tend to be a bit simpler to build and manage. After completing this book you should be able to evaluate the different business models and decide which one is right for you.

Now that we've covered enough of the basics to get started, let's move on to the next chapter and talk about how to quickly and effectively evaluate your product ideas.

CHAPTER 2:

VETTING IDEAS; HOW TO PICK A WINNER

The first trick to picking a winner is making sure you don't pick a loser. There are a few sure-fire ways to ensure you won't be successful, and you should do some work upfront to avoid landing on one of them. There are also a handful of ways to analyze the market and evaluate your product's potential before you start. We'll cover those here as well. It's also important to realize that a "winner" doesn't mean the same thing to every entrepreneur. Some might want to build a billion-dollar empire with thousands of employees while others are happy with a steady source of nearly-passive income. We'll talk about a few different business approaches so you can choose an idea that feels like a winner to you.

When thinking about bringing a product to market, one of the first things you should do is evaluate the feasibility of your idea. The customer will ultimately decide if your idea is a winner, but there are a few things you should consider from the outset to ensure you aren't doomed before you even start. In my experience the three biggest hurdles are economic feasibility, technical feasibility, and your personal ability to execute the idea with your current level of experience and expertise.

2.1: EVALUATING THE ECONOMIC FEASIBILITY OF YOUR IDEA:

Let's start with economic feasibility. The concept is really simple: If the customer isn't willing to pay enough for you to turn a worthwhile profit on your product, you don't have an economically feasible idea. This seems basic but it's often overlooked. If your product only solves a minor inconvenience or provides slight value for the customer, they probably won't pay hundreds of dollars for it. You need to step back and try to make an honest assessment on whether your product will be worth the price you need to charge. I find that economic feasibility kills more of my ideas than anything else.

In order to evaluate economic feasibility you first need to know how much your finished product will cost (MSRP). You can often formulate a pretty accurate guess by comparing your product to similar products already on the market, even if they're in vastly different categories. As an example, maybe you have a great idea for a massage therapy device that is molded from a single piece of hard rubber. While your exact product may not yet exist, you can probably find something similar on the shelves at a major retailer. You should look for items of similar material, construction, size, and complexity to yours for comparison. In this example, you might be able to find a solid rubber dog toy of similar size, material, and construction, retailing for $9.99. Since most companies have similar production costs and distribution networks, you can assume that the dog toy company is producing that toy for $2.00-$2.50. A production cost of $2.00-$2.50 means you'll need to price your product in the range of $10-$12.50 (remember our 500% markup starting point). If that seems like a reasonable price that customers would happily pay, you've passed the initial gut-check on economic feasibility.

2.2: EVALUATING THE TECHNICAL FEASIBILITY OF YOUR IDEA:

The next major hurdle is technical feasibility. As a design professional, I spent several years working in a department whose only job was to determine if various product ideas were technically feasible. We spent our days designing and building wacky Frankenstein prototypes to prove and test various concepts. At this stage you don't really care what the proof-of-concept prototypes look like – you can deal with that later. Your goal is to prove that you can, in fact, make a device that does what you want it to do. Another goal at this stage is to prove that the functioning device actually produces desirable results. I can't tell you how many times I've had an idea that seemed great, only to build a fully functional prototype and realize that the actual results aren't as fantastic as I expected.

You can often make quick functional prototypes by cobbling existing products together with some extra bits and pieces from the hardware store. If you need more specific hardware, McMaster.com is one of the most powerful resources on the planet. If you know CAD and have access to a 3D printer or CNC machine, that can also be a big help. Again, don't get caught up in making a slick prototype.

You want to answer the questions "Is this idea technically feasible" and "Is the outcome desirable" as quickly and cheaply as possible.

Some ideas are really simple and may not have any obvious technical challenges. Even if you're certain this is the case, I would still recommend making a functional prototype to ensure the outcome is desirable before you invest any more time or money. Even the simplest and most obvious-seeming solutions can often have unforeseen challenges or less-than-desirable outcomes.

Another aspect of technical feasibility is ensuring that you aren't infringing on someone else's patents. (As a quick disclaimer, I'm not an attorney and nothing in this book constitutes legal advice.) The first place to start is with a simple Google search. You want to find every product that is similar to your concept. When you find one, dig through their website to see if they list any patents. Most companies now use virtual patent marking to keep their product patent markings up to date, which means they maintain a comprehensive list of their patents somewhere on their website. If you can't readily find it online, check the product packaging because it should either contain the patent number or a URL to their virtual patent marking page if the device is patented.

The second place to search is Google Patents. Google has a dedicated patent search engine that is pretty powerful for the average Joe. You can search key product features or mechanisms and dig through the results until your heart's content. This isn't as comprehensive and accurate as some dedicated patent search programs the professionals use but it's a great start.

When you're reading patents, you're typically looking at the "claims" section. This is the part that matters most. If the claims seem to cover your invention, you might have an issue. Now, just because you don't see any obvious conflicts doesn't mean you're home free. There's an awful lot to know when reading and assessing patents, including information you may not have easy access to, like prosecution history. If you see anything that seems to remotely resemble your invention, it may be wise to get a "legal opinion" from an attorney before proceeding. A qualified patent attorney can do a detailed clearance search and provide their "opinion" on whether you have a conflict.

All in all, I try not to get too caught up in the legal aspect of the process. You can spend an extraordinary amount of time and money trying to understand the risk of infringement. There's also a very good chance your design will evolve during the development process, which may render your prior clearance search useless.

For the less risk-adverse readers among us, there is another commonly used method to approach IP infringement: Ignore it completely. (This seems like a great time to repeat that I'm not an attorney and nothing I say should be construed as legal advice.) I know of many successful product companies who take this approach. Having any certainty of IP clearance is so expensive and difficult that it can often be better to proceed without doing any formal IP research. The punishment can often be relatively minor if you infringe unknowingly, often just requiring that you stop selling the product. If you're willing to take the risk, this can be a viable strategy.

Most great new ideas don't pass the economic and technical feasibility tests, which is often the reason nobody else has already launched them! It's better to know sooner than later if your concept has a fundamental flaw that will prevent you from achieving success. Hopefully you have a whole list of potential ideas and you can quickly move on to the next when one proves unfeasible. On the bright side, you didn't spend months of time and thousands of dollars before you found the issue.

2.3: EVALUATING YOUR PERSONAL ABILITY TO EXECUTE YOUR IDEA

The last major hurdle is often a difficult pill to swallow. You need to consider whether you can realistically execute your product idea with your current level of experience, expertise, and the resources available to you. As a real-life example, I once decided to develop a medical device. I spent a lot of time and money developing this device and took it all the way to a patented, designed, functional prototype. It was a clever product with a significant market and the initial feedback from potential consumers was excellent. After I had the developed product in hand, I had no idea what to do next. Taking a medical device through the long and arduous process of FDA approval was well beyond my capability and vastly exceeded my available resources. I wasn't willing to spend 10 years and millions of dollars to get this device approved. I changed course and decided to try to sell the patent. I managed to get some initial interest from major pharmaceutical companies, but no takers. The idea died in a shoe box in my closet after many months of work and thousands of dollars invested. I didn't have the skillset and experience necessary to monetize this particular product. Unfortunately, this is a very common story among aspiring product entrepreneurs. This is why I recommend that people start with their simplest idea, especially if they have limited experience in bringing a product to market. Be honest when you evaluate your skillset. You might have the best idea ever for a new smartphone, but without some very specific experience, knowledge, and extensive resources, it's unlikely you can pull off a project of that complexity.

The best ideas are usually within your existing area of expertise. When you stick to what you know, you probably already understand the market and the customer's needs. You also might have insight on technical limitations and competitive solutions that an outsider does not. If you're a software engineer, for example, consider launching a mobile app instead of developing a physical product. You have a much higher chance of success if you work within an area where you already have some knowledge. Remember, you'll be competing with some extremely qualified and capable companies as you enter the market. If you go in knowing nothing, you might have a difficult time competing. Stick to what you know best whenever possible.

2.4: MARKET RESEARCH

Now that we've covered the three most common causes of spontaneous project death, let's shift our focus from avoiding the losers to picking winners.

"Will anyone buy my product?" This is the scary little question that haunts every product entrepreneur on every project, from conception to completion. You won't really be able to answer this question until you've made your first sale, but there are some ways to gauge the market potential before you even start.

First, look around for other products that are similar to yours. At this point in history, most problems or unmet consumer needs have been addressed to some degree. Your product may be better than what's already out there, but take the time to look at others that are addressing the same consumer need. A quick Google search for the competitive product should yield some telling results. Are a lot of well-known retailers selling the product? Are these retailers paying to advertise against that brand's keyword? If so, it might be a successful product. Retailers typically won't spend money on a net-negative ad campaign. If they're paying to advertise for a given product then it is most likely netting them a positive return on their ad spend. This is a telling sign of a successful product.

Amazon.com® can also be a great source of information at this stage. Take a look at the number of reviews on the competitive solution. Does it have a couple of reviews, or thousands? Something with only a couple of reviews may not have a very large market. Now, what about the quality of the reviews? Is this product pulling 5 stars across the board? If so, you might have a hard time stealing their customers. You should also scroll down the product page to the "Amazon Best Sellers Rank" and see where the product ranks in its category. All categories are different but if it has a top 50 ranking, odds are that the product is selling in decent volumes. This method can be a great initial check on sales volume but may not be conclusive. There are a lot of factors that vastly influence the sales volume on Amazon such as inconsistent inventory supply, improper product setup, lack of advertising, time the product has been listed on Amazon, etc. Just because a product isn't obviously selling well on Amazon doesn't mean they aren't successful elsewhere.

The next step is to get a bit more granular. Find the website of the competing company and paste their URL into in the "browse top sites" box on Alexa.com. Alexa.com is an Amazon-owned service that provides insights for professional marketers, but you can do a basic traffic search for free. This free report will give you a rough estimate on the amount of traffic the website receives, where that traffic comes from, similar sites, number of sites linking in, etc. If your competitor is a single-product company, this can be especially effective for gauging market size and customer interest. If they have an assortment of products, you really don't know which one(s) is generating the traffic so it is typically less valuable.

Sometimes you get lucky and can determine exactly how quickly a specific item is selling. Many brands and retailers track inventory on their website so they don't sell more than they have available. Try adding 9999 units to your cart and see if the website adjusts you down. They will often return a message saying "we only have 369 units available", for example. Record that number and the current time, then come back 24 hours later and do it again. Now it might say "we only have 354 units available" which means they most likely sold 15 units in the last 24 hours. You can try this on the company's own website, Amazon, or even sites of major retailers. You would be surprised at how much accurate data you can extract using this method.

At this point you may be wondering what to do if there are no products similar to your unique unicorn of an idea? Don't fret, there are still some great research options available. These still apply when there are competitive products available, by the way.

Google Trends and Google Keyword Planner are great resources for evaluating market potential. Google Trends shows you how search volumes for a given keyword or phrase have changed over time. There aren't hard search numbers within Google Trends, but you can see if the interest in your product category or the problem you're solving has increased or declined in recent years. Google Keyword Planner, on the other hand, will show you actual search volume of various keywords. As an example, you might be surprised to find out that in December of 2020 only 320 people searched for "heated ski jacket." If your big idea was to make a heated jacket for skiers, the existing market for your product might be much smaller than you would have expected. Depending on your goals, this might not be the market you want to approach due to the mild consumer interest.

You'll never be able to accurately guess what your sales will look like using the methods in this chapter, but it's certainly better than going in blind. If nothing else, you can usually get a sense of the opportunity that your product holds. Keep in mind that this research is far from foolproof. Occasionally, radical new ideas can go from zero to extraordinary scale in a very short timeframe. If you intend to solve a totally new problem or create value in a way nobody else saw possible, you would expect the number of existing solutions and keyword traffic to be extremely low. That doesn't necessarily mean the opportunity doesn't exist. These ideas are rare unicorns, but they do happen.

2.5: DEFINING SUCCESS FOR YOUR COMPANY

Now that you know how to avoid the losers and gauge the opportunity through research, you need to decide what a winning idea consists of in your world. As a product entrepreneur myself, I've gotten to know many others over the years. Some work just enough to maintain sales while their product generates enough consistent income for them to live comfortably. Others work non-stop with every intention of being the next billionaire. Both of these paths, and everything in between, are viable options for a product entrepreneur. It's highly unlikely that you'll become a billionaire while hardly working though, so go ahead and forget about that option.

Some markets, industries, and products are inherently more difficult than others. Making a complex product with enormous potential will require extraordinary efforts and commitment. If you don't want this process to consume your life, you might opt for doing something simpler with smaller potential. For example, let's look at the difference in starting Tesla and TubShroom. Tesla makes electric cars and TubShroom makes rubber drain plugs that catch hair before it goes down your shower drain. If you follow the stock market you probably know that Tesla has recently become one of the most valuable companies in the world, but this didn't come without extraordinary sacrifice and commitment from Elon Musk and a whole slew of other dedicated team members. On the other end of the spectrum, TubShroom made a simple product comprised of a single piece of molded rubber and they currently have over 71,000 Amazon reviews! TubShroom is probably generating a very nice annual income for the entrepreneur, and the work required to build and run that business is immeasurably small compared to Tesla. Both of these companies could be seen as winners depending on who is passing judgement. Would Elon be satisfied with running TubShroom? Probably not. Would you? Possibly. This is what you need to decide and you should choose the product idea you pursue accordingly.

CHAPTER 3:

REFINING YOUR CONCEPT THROUGH BRANDING

At this point in the process you should have an economically and technically feasible product idea that you can realistically execute with your own experience level. You may feel ready to put rubber to the road and start making your product a reality, but you're getting ahead of yourself. It's no longer enough to simply make a functional product that provides value or solves a problem. Customers have choices now and, if you don't have direct competition when you launch, just give it a year. Knockoffs, copies, and even counterfeits will come out of the woodwork and undercut your price. Your best defense is good branding.

Branding is much more than a name and a logo. It's how you portray the identity and values of your company to your customer. When done correctly, branding should play a role in every aspect of your product business including: Defining the features of the product itself, the aesthetic design decisions of the product and packaging, the colorways you choose to offer, the language you use in written product descriptions, the style of photography, your website layout, and virtually every other decision that is associated with the product and its presentation to the customer. Your branding should be a major guiding force in your decision making process from this point forward.

3.1: DEFINING YOUR TARGET CUSTOMER

In order to effectively use branding to guide your decisions, you first need to develop your brand and understand what it's all about. I recommend starting with your target consumer. If you're making a new baby stroller, perhaps your target customer is new moms, age 22-34. If you're designing a new power tool, your target customer might be a 45-year-old male construction foreman. As you can imagine, these two customers have very different needs, desires, and goals. They want their products to look and feel a certain way. In the case of these two, nearly everything about the brands should be different: Colors, aesthetic design, packaging, messaging, photography style, all of it!

It's not enough to simply dial in the age, gender, and lifestyle of your target consumer. You should really build out an entire persona. In marketing, this is often called a "muse." Your muse is your absolute ideal customer. This is the person you work to please the most. When building out the persona of your muse, go ahead and give them a name. Start with demographics like age, sex, income, profession, where they live, height, and weight. Then move into psychographics like their hobbies, interests, favorite movies, fears, hopes, dreams, etc. You want to know your muse as well as you know a good friend.

Once you have a full persona developed, write a one-paragraph elevator pitch of your product in a style that will appeal to this customer. Then try to narrow that down to a single sentence. Both will be useful going forward. Let's look at an example of how the copywriting for the same product may differ for two different customers. In this example, we'll use the same two personas previously mentioned: A 25-year-old new mother and a 45-year-old male construction foreman. Let's pretend you've developed a new aloe-infused moisturizing bar soap that works wonders on dry skin while still providing a deep clean.

Example 1:

"Our aloe-infused bar soap provides a deep, gentle clean and all-day moisture to keep you looking and feeling your best."

Example 2:

"Our aloe-infused bar soap helps repair dry and damaged skin without sacrificing the cleaning power you need after a long day."

Can you tell which line was intended for which customer?

In this example we kept the product exactly the same and simply framed it in two different ways to appeal to our core customer. But if you're really doing your job as a product entrepreneur, you'll go a step further. Now that you truly know your customer and what they value, you should tailor the product to fit their needs from the very beginning of the project. Let's continue with the bar soap example: If you want to make a bar soap brand that really appeals to the 45-year-old male construction foreman, you need to do a bit more than just align the copywriting with their values. You need to align the product and brand as well. Perhaps the bar soap comes in different scents like cedar-citrus and aloe-pine. These would both smell great without being too flowery or perfumy for your muse. Maybe you include a little ground pumice stone in the soap that helps clean the dirt from the cracks in their hand and elicits memory of the industrial-strength hand soaps they find on job sites. When designing the shape of the soap bar, you could give it some hard angles that make it look a bit more masculine than a traditional bar of soap which usually has soft, rounded styling. The bar itself could be oversized because your muse is 6'4" tall and would appreciate the larger bar. The packaging could be a simple recycled cardboard box with a wax seal at the closure, paying homage to the wax seal on high-end whiskey bottles. All of this should be considered on every product you develop from the very beginning, and it all starts by crafting a detailed customer persona.

3.2: SELECTING YOUR TARGET RETAILERS

Another thing that you should consider as you start to define and refine your product idea is who your target retail accounts will be. By this, I'm referring to the stores where you would like to sell your products. A product that sells in Home Depot should probably look and feel much different than a similar product that will be sold at Target. On average, these two stores have very different customers walking their aisles and they go to great lengths to ensure the products on their shelves appeal to this customer. If you plan to land your product in a specific retailer, you should have their customer in mind from the get-go. The best way to do this is by aligning your muse with the core customer of your dream retail account. Working more off the soap bar example, you can probably imagine the soap bar we just described being sold in the checkout line at the Home Depot or ACE Hardware, but probably not at Target or Bed Bath & Beyond. Thinking about your ideal retail placement should provide more incentive to carefully craft your muse and ensure the persona you develop aligns with your future vision of the product.

Your colorways and packaging design will also be highly influenced by your retailers of choice. I recommend you spend some time walking the aisles of different stores, noting the different colors of the products on their shelves, the different packaging types, and how products are displayed within the store. The way a brand or product is presented in a store is called "merchandising" and having the right merchandising can make all the difference in whether your product gets selected to be sold in a retail store. Your product and packaging should look at home on the shelves of your target retail accounts. If it doesn't, you hardly stand a chance of selling in.

If you haven't been through the process a few times, it may not be immediately apparent how you would design a product or brand to appeal to a specific customer. Building an inspiration board can be a helpful exercise to guide you through the process. To build an inspiration board you should put together a collage of images and copy from products and brands that do an excellent job of targeting your core customer. Continuing with the example of the bar soap for construction foremen, I would include images of Ridgid power tools and RedWing boots, high-end bourbon packaging, written copy from the Carhart website, possibly some inspiration from Yeti coolers and other like-minded brands. By combining all this information into a single document, you can easily leverage the work done by other brands who already do an excellent job of appealing to your core customer. You should have great examples of how to stylize your product, what the packaging could look like, and what the written copy should sound like. This step is used by professional marketers all the time, but it's even more important for people with no experience in branding.

3.3: NAMING YOUR PRODUCT AND BRAND

Another critical part of branding is choosing a name. I'd recommend waiting until you're a little closer to launching your product before you decide on a name (a lot can change in the development process), but when it comes time to choose a name for your product you definitely need to keep your muse in mind. There's a lot to consider when choosing a name such as: Is it already being used, is it a commonly used word or phrase that will make you difficult to find in search results, is it memorable, does it appeal to your core customer, will you have issues down the road for cultural or social appropriation or lack of political correctness, and so much more. Choosing a great name is more of an art than a science, so try to think through all the angles as you narrow your selections.

One thing you will need to do before committing to a name is ensure nobody else in your space is already using it. A quick Google search is a good place to start. If you're making bar soap and the only other person using your name makes business software, you're probably ok to proceed. However, if you're making bar soap and someone else is using the name on their laundry detergent, you probably have an issue.

With trademarks, the date the name was first used commercially is often the most important deciding factor in who has rights to the mark. If someone beat you to it, you should look for a different name.

The next place you'll want to search is the USPTO TESS online database. This is the official database of registered trademarks across the U.S. It is relatively simple to use but may require some knowledge and experience to decipher the results. Trademarks typically apply to specific categories of product so if someone has a similar name in a similar product category you should probably opt to use a different name. It's worth noting that tweaking the spelling is not enough to prevent infringement if it is phonetically the same. This is a common mistake. As an example, perhaps you want to use the name "YetiSuds" for your manly soap brand but you see that it's already taken so you decide to use "Yeti Sudz" instead. Unfortunately, that doesn't cut it.

Only names that have been registered with the USPTO will show up in the TESS database. Just because a name hasn't been registered doesn't mean it's up for grabs.

You're probably familiar with both the "trademark" and "registered trademark" symbols, ™ and ® respectively. Only the registered trademark has been registered with the government. The TM mark is more of an informal claim indicating that the mark is intended to be unique to your brand and you intend to protect it going forward. You can use this one for free, but be careful not to step on other brands using the simple TM mark. You typically need to prove commercial use before you can formally register a trademark, so you'll likely start with the free TM mark anyways.

Another consideration you might want to include when naming your brand is the availability of web URL addresses and social media handles. You probably want your brand name to align with your .com and your social media @ name, so choosing something unique can be favorable. This has become increasingly difficult in recent years so it's very common to include descriptors like YetiSudsSoap.com instead of just YetiSuds.com. This doesn't seem to have any major adverse effects so long as it is done well.

3.4: DEVELOPING YOUR LOGO

Once you have a name, you're ready to develop a logo. Your logo could be an icon, a wordmark, or a combination of both. You will probably need to hire a professional to produce your logo if you don't have a design background. There are some really affordable options like Fiverr.com where you can get a basic logo design done for $5, to 99designs.com where you should expect to pay a few hundred dollars for some pretty nice results, on to professional consultancies that will gladly charge you thousands or tens-of-thousands of dollars to develop an excellent logo to pair with your brand identity. When designing a logo, keep your muse in mind. This needs to be something that they won't mind having stamped on the side of their product. It also needs to be something you'll be proud to wear on a t-shirt or hat at a tradeshow in the future. A few technical notes: Ensure your logo still looks ok when it's printed in a single color. There will be applications where black and white printing is the only option. Ensure it can be printed very small or very large without losing too much detail to be legible. You'll also want to get both raster and vector files of your logo. The vector files will be necessary for scaling your logo up in the future, or applying it to product and packaging. Any qualified designer should be familiar with these terms and should happily provide both file types upon request.

CHAPTER 4:

GETTING STARTED; THE BORING STUFF

Now that you've done your homework by researching the market opportunity and proving the feasibility of your project, you should be ready to commit and get started. Unfortunately, getting started requires some pretty boring paperwork and business setup. Let's walk through some of the basic tasks required to set up your business and operate efficiently. Keep in mind that I'm not an attorney, this isn't legal advice, and the goal here is to provide a very brief overview so you know the next steps. At minimum you should do some additional research of your own, or you can hire a corporate attorney to advise and assist with business setup.

4.1: REGISTERING YOUR BUSINESS

Making and selling products typically comes with some inherent liability. If someone gets hurt using your product, they could attempt to sue you personally. You should set up a corporation or disregarded entity to minimize the liability to your personal assets. There are a variety of options available to you in the United States, and each one has different requirements and different taxation treatments. I've outlined the most common types in the following paragraphs, but I typically advise most product entrepreneurs to file a standard LLC for their balance of simplicity, flexibility, and liability protection.

A Sole Proprietorship (or a Partnership if there are multiple owners) is the simplest business type but typically does not provide any protection for your personal assets in a liability suit. This may be ok if you're selling handmade jewelry on Etsy.com but likely isn't a good choice if you have bigger plans. You will typically use your social security number instead of an EIN (employer identification number) on most legal and tax documents. You may not need to register your sole proprietorship or partnership but you might need to register a trade name (Also called a DBA for "Doing Business As") or obtain a business license depending on your industry and/or location.

An LLC is a very common and versatile option for business registration, and it's the one I recommend to most product entrepreneurs. The LLC works well for a single owner, partners, or a business with any number of owners. The LLC is commonly referred to as a "pass-through entity" because the company's income is typically taxed as the owners' income. The profits simply "pass through" to the owner. This is simple to operate but it does not carry a lot of tax benefits. The LLC does theoretically provide liability protection for your personal assets by separating the company as a disregarded entity from the owner(s). Note that you'll want to put an "operating agreement" in place if you have more than a single owner/member in your LLC. This may also be required for a single member LLC in some locations. You might be able to find a simple operating agreement template online that will meet your needs, but if you plan to have a partner or multiple members in your LLC, it may be best to have an attorney construct this document in case you and your partner(s) have a falling-out down the road. With an LLC you will register your business with the state and you'll receive an EIN (employer identification number) from the federal government that you can use on most legal and tax documents. This also provides some additional personal privacy over a sole proprietorship because you won't have to use your personal social security number for your business dealings.

A C Corporation may be the best choice if you plan to raise capital or take your company public someday. Owners are technically "shareholders" in this arrangement and it allows for the issuance of preferred stock which is often appealing for early investors. C Corps also provide liability protection like an LLC. On the downside, the setup requires significantly more legwork and there are more rules and requirements for managing a C Corp. As an example, a board of directors is required, as are regular meetings and detailed record keeping. You will probably want to consult an attorney before electing to register as a C Corp.

The S Corporation is another one you hear a lot about, though this is technically a tax classification rather than a business type. Either an LLC or a Corporation can elect to be taxed as an S Corp. The S Corp. carries the liability protection of either the LLC or Corporation that it is registered as, but the owners can elect to be taxed as employees instead of paying self-employment taxes. This can carry some taxation benefits for some companies or owners. The downside of an S Corp. often comes in their lack of flexibility and more stringent rules. S Corps are typically required to have a board of directors and there are regular meeting requirements that must be upheld. You might want to consult an accountant and possibly a business attorney before deciding to set up an S Corp.

Registering a business usually starts by filing "Articles of Organization" with your state. A good number of companies choose to register their company in Delaware instead of their home state because they see larger companies do it, but this may or may not make sense for you. Large companies typically register in Delaware because Delaware has a special court with expert business judges so companies don't become victim to a traditional jury in a suit or dispute. If this isn't important to you, you might consider registering in your home state to keep things simple.

If you plan to have employees in the future, you can apply for an EIN (Employer Identification Number) with the IRS on their website. This is like a social security number for your business. It will be used on many legal and tax documents in the future so keep good track of it after you get it.

You need to name your company in order to register it with the government. Don't overthink this step – this doesn't have to be the name you'll use publicly in the future. Many entrepreneurs will give the company a generic name for registration purposes. If your last name is Albertson, you can name your company Albertson Products LLC or something equally simple. Once you launch your actual brand name you can register that as a DBA (Doing Business As) and use that as your public-facing name. If your future brand name ends up being ProDrive, you may refer to your company as Albertson Products LLC dba ProDrive. This won't cause you any hardship in the future. It's actually extremely common, so don't get caught up on naming your company at the time of registration. You can file a DBA registration with your state at any time in the future.

4.2: OPENING A BUSINESS BANK ACCOUNT AND CREDIT CARD

Once you get your business registered, you should consider opening a dedicated business bank account. This will help you track expenses for tax purposes and will start to build some business history. Consider going with a national banking chain who can support the needs of the larger business you hope to become in the future. Be sure to put your business name and your DBA name on the bank account. Note that you can always add your DBA name later if you don't know it at this point.

Your next step is to get a business credit card with reward points. This will help you build a credit history for your company and provide some additional financial benefits. American Express has some great options with increased rewards in specific categories like shipping and advertising. This can be a very nice income source for you as your business grows. A small to medium size business can often have hundreds of thousands of dollars in monthly expenses, and putting those on a credit card with 1%-3% rewards can be very lucrative on these large amounts. There is often no extra fee to pay your expenses with a credit card vs other forms of payment so the rewards are free to you. I personally try to choose cards that give me rewards at places I would shop anyways. This basically becomes free income and effectively reduces your expenses by 1%-3% whenever you use the card. This may seem like a strange recommendation this early in the business process, but do the math and you'll quickly realize why getting a good rewards card should be such a high priority for any business owner.

4.3: SHIPPING ACCOUNTS

Next up on the list, you'll want to set up a shipping account with a major courier. FedEx and UPS are the two obvious options in the U.S. and you typically get a significant rate discount just for signing up for an account online. This alone will save you time and money, but you'll also be able to ship on other companies' accounts and have them ship on your account in the future. This is a common business practice and it's nice to look like you know what you're doing when interacting with other businesses. Once you have a favorite carrier, you'll want to shift the vast majority of your shipping volume to that carrier to increase your shipping volume with them. As your shipping volumes increase you should get in touch with your local rep to negotiate improved shipping rates. It's not uncommon to get discounts of 75% or more on premium services once you have some volume. This results in massive savings and is a total necessity if you want to be competitive with other businesses in your industry.

You'll also want to set up an account with Stamps.com so you can easily print postage to ship via USPS (postal service). The Postal Service still has, by far, the cheapest shipping on packages under 13 ounces in the U.S. and 4 lbs internationally. They're also the go-to for mailing documents, letters, and checks, so it's very nice to be able to print postage digitally. A Stamps.com account will enable you to do all these things quickly, easily, and affordably.

4.4: SALES TAX LICENSE

You'll eventually need to apply for your sales tax licenses but I recommend you hold off on doing this until you're about to start selling product. This process became significantly more complicated in the last few years since most states started requiring out-of-state sellers to pay sales tax if they meet certain criteria. You'll have to do your own research on those requirements because those laws are always changing. Even if you don't meet the requirements to be taxed as an out-of-state seller, you will probably need to file sales tax in your home city and state plus anywhere else you have a physical or economic presence. When you first start selling you likely won't have an economic presence anywhere you don't have a physical presence. A physical presence includes anywhere you have an office, employees, or inventory. A quick web search for your city or state followed by "sales tax" will point you in the right direction for getting signed up with an account. I strongly recommend using a plugin on your website called TaxJar to help you stay compliant with the complex sales tax laws throughout the U.S. With proper setup this app can automate all your tax filings and payments. With the absurd complexity of the sales tax system in the U.S., it is nearly impossible to maintain compliance in a fast-growing business without some good software to assist you.

4.5: LIABILITY INSURANCE

Product liability insurance is another not-so-fun task that you don't need to tackle immediately but should strongly consider obtaining before you actually sell anything. These policies are intended to protect your company in the instance that someone is hurt through the use or misuse of your product. We've all heard about the ridiculous lawsuits that get filed against companies and this policy will help cover your costs and losses if you're on the wrong end of one of those suits. A quick web search for "Product liability insurance near me" should yield some useful results of local agencies who can get you a plan from a reputable underwriter. I recommend getting your policy through a company who has been in business for a long time and that you've heard of before, like The Hartford. This will help ensure you actually get the coverage you expect. These policies can be hundreds of pages long so, unless you're an expert at evaluating business insurance policies, you probably need to choose a quality underwriter whom you can trust to treat you right.

As your business grows and you start to sell your product into various retailers, these retailers will typically require proof that you have adequate product liability insurance before they will carry your product. The most common insurance requirement to work with most major retailers is currently $2,000,000 per occurrence and $4,000,000 aggregate. You will need a policy that has at least these limits to be eligible to work with most major retailers. They will typically request a certificate of insurance, also known as a COI, during the vendor setup process. This is a document you acquire through your insurance provider that lists the retailer as an "additional insured" and clearly states the coverage limits. With most good policies these certificates are provided for free upon request.

As with all things in business, timing is important. I highly recommend completing these steps as needed instead of doing them all at once before they're necessary. For example, you'll need to have a registered business in order to open a business bank account, but there's no reason to open a business bank account until you're ready to start spending money on your idea. Open your shipping accounts once you start shipping samples and prototypes, but not before you've registered your business. Secure your sales tax licenses and liability insurance shortly before you start selling product, but not before you've manufactured the product you intend to sell. This whole process is about doing the right work at the right time because your time as an entrepreneur is extremely limited and must be used properly. Be careful not to put the cart before the horse. For example, don't sign up for sales tax licenses before you've even finished development on your product. That may prove to be a total waste of time and money if your product doesn't come to fruition – time that could have been better spent developing a different idea that will come to fruition. Refer to Chapter 14 if you need a chronological outline of the proper order to execute these various tasks.

CHAPTER 5:

FINANCING YOUR PRODUCT BUSINESS

Product development is expensive. Engineering and design work are expensive. Molds and tooling are expensive. Inventory is expensive. These are all challenges that make running a product-based business more difficult than most other types of businesses. To head off this challenge, you need to develop a plan for how you intend to finance your product business so you don't stall out when it comes time to put your money where your mouth is. You also need to ensure your financing strategy aligns with your vision of the future for your company. Your strategy will be different if you want to build a company that will produce consistent profits for decades vs. wanting to grow an organization extremely quickly in hopes of getting acquired. Your end goals should play a driving role in your financing strategy.

There are a few common strategies for financing a product business. My personal favorite is "bootstrapping." Bootstrapping is where the entrepreneur puts up a small initial investment themselves and grows the business entirely from the profits it generates. Other common tactics include debt financing, equity financing, and crowdfunding. All of these have their upsides and downsides which we'll discuss briefly in this chapter. The most important thing is that you develop a realistic funding strategy that aligns with your resources, abilities, and goals.

5.1: BOOTSTRAPPING

Let's start with bootstrapping. This is my personal favorite for a number of reasons and I recommend this method for most aspiring product entrepreneurs. If you have some savings and you don't mind the risk, bootstrapping provides the least resistance to getting started. You are the only person standing in your way. Once your bootstrapped company is operating, you don't have a boss because you don't have any investors. You're free to do things exactly how you like and nobody can tell you otherwise. You maintain full ownership of your company so you get all the upside when you're successful. Most importantly, successfully bootstrapping a product company requires extreme discipline and high-quality management practices that will result in a strong, lean organization. You can't bootstrap a profitable product company with sloppy business practices. Of the product companies I've seen start and die over the last decade, the bootstrapped companies have lasted longer and weathered storms much better than similar equity-financed or crowd-funded companies.

Bootstrapping doesn't come without its downsides, and the biggest of these may be stress. You're risking a significant chunk of your own life savings when you choose to bootstrap a product company, and that's more than enough to keep most people awake at night. Growing a business on only your own profits is also difficult and stressful. As your sales increase, you'll likely need more inventory to support the increased sales. You're left trying to pay your expenses, pay your staff, pay your taxes, pay yourself, grow your business, and invest in more inventory all from the incoming profits. Managing cash flow under these parameters can be a beast of a job. Depending on your margins and growth rate, you may find that your ability to grow is restricted by your cashflow when bootstrapping. This should be a consideration if your goal is to grow your business as quickly as possible. If you reach this point where growth is restricted by cash flow, you can always seek additional funding to get you over the hump. One of the beautiful things about bootstrapping is that you aren't locked into the bootstrapping strategy forever just because that's how you start.

With all that said, I firmly believe bootstrapping produces the strongest companies and I recommend it to most aspiring entrepreneurs who have the available resources to pull it off. If you don't have the savings available, you may be able to start in a similar way with debt financing.

5.2: DEBT FINANCING

Debt financing as a small business will typically be structured as a loan that you pay back with interest. This can be very difficult to acquire for a new, unproven business so you'll probably have to back the loan with a personal guarantee. Depending on your situation, you may also want to explore some less obvious channels than a traditional bank loan. To make debt financing work, you need to convince someone to believe in you and your idea enough to loan you a significant amount of seed money with long repayment terms. Product companies are not quick to start and they take even longer to begin generating a profit, so you might not be able to pay back a single dime for a year or two even if you're successful. If you do have a personal guarantee on your loan, this strategy comes with all the stress of traditional bootstrapping but now with expensive principal and interest payments to add to that stress. On the upside, if you pull it off you get all the benefits of a bootstrapped business including full ownership, full autonomy, no boss, and the opportunity to build a lean and disciplined organization.

5.3: EQUITY FINANCING

If neither of these options seem ideal, or if your vision is to grow your company very quickly to attract a potential buyer, taking outside investment may be the best way forward for you. Acquisitions are very common in some industries if you can gain significant traction in the market, so this can be a valid business model. You frequently see this model used in Silicon Valley with new apps or software startups – they have no intention of ever turning a profit on their own, instead hoping to disrupt the industry enough to get bought. If this is your strategy, you'll need some serious cash injected from an outside source.

Raising capital in these high-risk-high-reward companies is most frequently done by selling equity. You are essentially selling part of the company for money to start or grow the company. In the beginning, before you have a proven product, you can expect to trade a lot of ownership for a relatively small amount of money. After all, you're just a person with an idea and you haven't really done anything of value yet, so there's no reason anyone would pay a lot of money for a stake in your unproven company. As you make progress, start generating revenue, and generally prove yourself and your product, you will theoretically be able to sell each remaining percentage point of your company for a higher value. This is often the most effective funding technique if you have a very big idea that will require a lot of capital to get off the ground, or if you need to grow extremely quickly to gain brand recognition before the competition copies your product.

Equity investments can come from a variety of places including venture capital firms, angel investors, friends and family, or really any person or organization that wants to buy a stake in your company. Depending on the investor and the type of share you sell, understand that you may be hiring yourself a boss. These people gave you their hard-earned money and they will want to receive frequent updates on how you're using it. They'll also want constant status updates on your progress, financial reports, and they'll want to see you generating revenue as quickly as possible. They may even want to tell you how to run your business and weigh in on important decisions. This should be a major consideration for the entrepreneur since many of us want to start a company for the increased independence, only to trade that back for the capital to get it off the ground. This system also has the tendency to produce bloated, wasteful companies. You do not have to be lean and effective to survive when cash is being injected from outside sources. Funded companies often spend frivolously and sometimes launch half-baked products under pressure from the investors.

On the upside, funded companies can accomplish things that bootstrapped companies simply can't do. They can often achieve bigger goals that may not have a positive return for a decade or more. They can use their deep pockets to gain market share and grow revenues extremely quickly. They can disrupt entire industries by innovating faster than the incumbents and stealing away customers. They can do enough damage and garner enough attention to attract an acquisition in a relatively short amount of time. If that is your goal and you aren't deterred by the downsides, this may be the best funding strategy for your business.

If you plan to raise capital through equity investment, you need to structure your company accordingly. As mentioned in section 4.1, a C Corporation is likely the best entity type for selling equity. You will also need all the accompanying documentation to sell equity including: Articles of incorporation, shareholder agreement, bylaws, stock certificates, etc. Properly registering your C Corporation and generating these documents is a complex job that should be done by a qualified corporate attorney.

You will need a formal business plan to raise funds through equity financing. This is the document you'll use to pitch your business to potential investors. A business plan acts as a detailed outline of your strategy to launch, grow, and monetize your business. There is so much documentation available on building business plans that it's hardly worth covering in this book. A quick Google search will yield hundreds of instructional articles for you to reference on the topic. There are also dozens books dedicated to building business plans. I recommend you do your research and follow the format outlined by these experts.

5.4: CROWDFUNDING

Crowdfunding is another method that is commonly used to get product companies off the ground. This is often done using a platform like Kickstarter or Indiegogo. With crowdfunding, the product is essentially pre-sold to the customer before it is ever manufactured. The proceeds go toward the development, tooling, and first production run of the product. This is a brilliant idea in theory, but only occasionally works out in practice. There have been a handful of successful product companies that started via crowdfunding, but the long-term failure rate of companies that successfully crowdfunded is astounding.

If you choose to use crowdfunding to finance your product, do so with relative caution. You should use crowdfunding purely as a source of financing and not an indication of future sales potential. Products that succeed on crowdfunding sites do not often succeed in the real world, and vice versa. This is because real-world shoppers aren't willing to watch 6-minute videos on the next new gadget with 47 features. Real-world shoppers are busy and they're only willing to give a millisecond of their attention to something if it seems like it will provide significant value or solve an immediate problem in their lives. Additionally, crowdfunding platforms attract early adopters who like trying out unproven technology. Early adopters make up a very small percentage of the overall population. The fact that your product can sell to a thoroughly curated group of bored early adopters on a crowdfunding site does not mean that your product will sell to the rest of the world. I've heard many horror stories of entrepreneurs who invested heavily in inventory after a very successful crowdfunding campaign, only to watch their sales go to zero after their product entered the traditional market. They often get stuck with hundreds of thousands of dollars of unwanted inventory, no cash, and the companies fail.

Don't get me wrong, crowdfunding can be a very effective funding tool if used properly. It's a great way to finance your product company without giving up equity, taking on debt, or even investing your own money. In reality, it may be the best way to finance most product ideas. The danger comes in also using the results of the crowdfunding campaign as market research. This works both ways where products that are successfully crowdfunded fail to translate to the real world, but also vice versa. As a real-life example, I once tried to crowdfund a very simple product idea that I thought was interesting but just wasn't certain about. It failed to fund. A few years later I decided to launch it anyways and that idea became one of the fastest selling products I've ever managed. In fact, it became one of the fastest selling items in a national retail store chain! If I had let the crowdfunding results drive my decision making, I never would have launched that successful product. Crowdfunding can be great but be sure to use it for what it is – funding.

Funding becomes much easier to find after you have some business success. Lenders will come out of the woodwork to loan you money. Many of the financial service companies and sales platforms you use to conduct business may offer you loans, including PayPal, Amazon, Shopify, QuickBooks, and American Express. Your bank may call to offer you a revolving line of credit and Amex may give you a credit card with no limit. Potential equity investors will inquire by phone and email on a weekly basis. What was once difficult to come by can become difficult to escape. The increased availability of these funding options means that you can change your financing strategy along the way as you find success. Just because you start with one financial strategy doesn't mean you're stuck with it. Your financial needs will change drastically as your business grows and markets develop, so keep an open mind and consider altering your financial strategy as your needs change. Just make sure to maintain a high degree of financial discipline as all these avenues of easy money open up to you.

CHAPTER 6:

ACCOUNTING AND TAXES

We're about to get to the fun stuff soon, but there's just a little bit more of the not-so-fun stuff to cover before we move on. Now that you've developed a funding strategy and have some money in your business, you need to start tracking it. The process of tracking and documenting the movement of money throughout your business is called "bookkeeping" and you need to start doing this immediately. Why the rush? Because proper bookkeeping from the very beginning of your project will likely save you a ton of money on your taxes. Now I'm no accountant, but I'm pretty sure that any entrepreneur worth their salt can get on board with reducing their tax burden.

6.1: TAX DEDUCTIBLE BUSINESS EXPENSES

All the money you spend on qualifying business expenses can be deducted from your taxable income. This means you won't have to pay taxes on that portion of your revenue. Most product companies spend 75% or more of their total income on business expenses, so you're going to lose out in a big way if you don't properly track and deduct these expenses.

6.2: LEARNING ACCOUNTING BASICS

In addition to tracking expenses, you also need to track your initial investment. After all, you don't want to pay taxes on the money you put in to start your company since you probably paid tax on it when you earned it the first time. You'll also want to be able to track your sales, see who owes you money, pay bills on time, manage and understand your cashflow, produce and read a balance statement, comprehend a profit and loss statement (P&L), and other basic accounting stuff that every entrepreneur should know. If you aren't already familiar with everything I just mentioned, you have some homework to do.

Accounting and bookkeeping are complex subjects that require years of study and practice to master. Fortunately you don't have to master them to get by as a product entrepreneur, but you do need to gain a basic understanding. I strongly recommend that you buy and study a book called *The Accounting Game: Basic Accounting Fresh from the Lemonade Stand* by Darrell Mullis and Judith Orloff. This is literally the most valuable book I have ever read as a product entrepreneur. It's an absolute essential if the world of accounting and bookkeeping is foreign to you.

As you'll learn in *The Accounting Game*, a product company with inventory must use accrual-based accounting. In short, this means that expenses and income are accounted for when they are incurred, not when the money actually changes hands. Tracking all of this can become laborious pretty quickly, especially if you're selling wholesale to accounts with payment terms like Net60. "Net60" means that you ship the product and send the invoice today but the account has 60 days to actually pay the bill (We'll discuss payment terms in detail in section 12.1). With accrual accounting, you don't get to wait until the money is received before you consider it to be income. It is considered income from the date of the invoice. You then need to watch for the actual payment to hit your bank account and match that payment to the open invoice so you know who has paid and who hasn't. You also need to know who is late on payment and who isn't due yet. Can you see how this can quickly get complicated once you have a few dozen wholesale accounts? Now scale that up to hundreds or thousands of accounts and you have a real mess on your hands!

6.3: BOOKKEEPING AND ACCOUNTING SOFTWARE

To organize the mess, track expenses, make financial reporting easy, and generally manage the finances of your business, I recommend adopting an accounting software like QuickBooks. I personally prefer QuickBooks Online due to the simple interface, cloud security and storage, seamless integrations with other web platforms, and the ability to connect from anywhere on any computer. Now let's get one thing straight; QuickBooks won't do you a bit of good if you don't have a decent understanding of accounting terms and bookkeeping processes. Before you even bother setting up an accounting software for your business, you should read *The Accounting Game.* I can't repeat that statement enough.

As an alternative to learning how to keep your own books, you can hire a bookkeeper. I typically recommend that entrepreneurs do it themselves for a year or two first to learn the process and understand how it all works. If you aren't up for that then sure, you can hire someone else to do it. Depending on the workflow and complexity of your books, this may or may not ultimately save you time each week. QuickBooks Online has some pretty great automations with customizable rules and it can often be faster to categorize your own expenses rather than explain them all to someone else who then categorizes them for you, especially when it's just you and a small handful of employees. As the company grows, you'll probably want someone else to manage the bookkeeping.

6.4: BUSINESS TAXES

Your end-of-year taxes are a different story. You will definitely want to hire a professional accountant to close out your books for the year and prepare your taxes. The way you prepare and file your taxes will depend on the type of business you registered and your taxation elections. A qualified accountant will know how to handle your unique situation properly. A great accountant will do more than just prepare your taxes, though. They will help you minimize your tax burden and identify ways you can further minimize this burden in the future. They may even have other suggestions on how to manage the finances of your company to maximize your profits or improve efficiency. Every great business needs a great accountant.

If you're filing taxes as a self-employed individual, which is extremely common among LLC owners, you are expected to pay estimated "quarterly" taxes. I put that in quotation marks because the payment schedule is typically a little off from a true quarterly schedule. 2021 due dates for these payments are the 15th of April, June, September, and January. You probably won't know exactly how much is due for each period but if you underpay by too much you will be penalized. Your accountant should give you an estimate of your upcoming quarterly payments based on the prior year and, if you maintain that payment schedule, you will not be penalized. You'll typically avoid penalty if you owe less than $1,000 at the end of the year, if you paid 90% of the tax due for the year via quarterly payments, or if you paid 100% of the tax amount from the prior year. You'll still have to pay any remaining balance, but hitting these marks will typically help you avoid paying additional penalties. You can pay your estimated quarterly tax payments on the IRS.GOV website.

6.5: FINANCIAL MANAGEMENT OF INVENTORY

While we're talking about accounting, let's quickly cover the topic of inventory. Inventory is a necessary evil for product companies and you typically want to hold as little inventory as possible without negatively impacting sales. In most product companies the cost of goods sold (this is inventory that has been sold) is the largest single expense. You may also find that you have more money in inventory than you have in the bank most of the time. This happens for a variety of reasons but the biggest contributor is that production lead times on physical products are often 90 days or more. If you manufacture overseas then you also have to ship the goods after production which can often take 6 additional weeks or more. The primary goal of your inventory is to absorb sales fluctuations since you can't quickly adjust to changes in demand with these long lead times. Even if you don't have fluctuations, you still need some inventory to cover the periods between production runs.

Inventory is bad for a number of reasons. First and foremost, inventory is expensive and money that's sitting in inventory is not helping you grow your business. As a product entrepreneur you need to use the money you have to make more money. This is commonly called "working capital." If all your money is sitting in a warehouse, it isn't working for you – it's just stuck there until you sell the product. Second, inventory does not always sell. You may invest heavily only to find out that people don't want what you're selling. This is essentially lost money if you can't recoup your costs by selling at a discount. Third, inventory can become outdated, defective, damaged, or undesirable over time. Reference reason two if you don't already know why this is a bad thing.

Inventory is evil, but it's a necessary evil. As we just discussed, you probably need some level of inventory to cover sales fluctuations and provide you with something to sell between production runs. The trick is holding just the right amount of inventory to achieve these goals without running out or buying too much. This is one of the most important and difficult tasks within a product-based company. A small mistake on inventory can result in lost revenue or a lack of working capital, and both of those can be very bad things.

The most important takeaway from this chapter is that you need to start tracking the movement of money through your business by bookkeeping. If you don't know what you're doing in the realm of accounting and bookkeeping, do your homework and learn the basics before you start. I realize this stuff isn't exciting and probably isn't why you're interested in starting a company, but it's all very, very important to your future success.

CHAPTER 7:

BRINGING YOUR PRODUCT TO LIFE

It took six chapters to get here, but here we are – ready to start working on the actual product! At this point you should have already built a proof-of-concept prototype that proved your concept is technically feasible and produces a desirable outcome. You've also outlined your target customer and built an inspiration board of existing products that do a great job of appealing to this customer. The next step is to fit all those wonderful components and features from your proof-of-concept prototype into a tidy product package that looks and feels like the products on your inspiration board. Then you have to design that product for mass production and ensure that it meets all legal and regulatory requirements. If you're not an expert in the fields of mechanical engineering, industrial design, or general product development, consider outsourcing this part of the project. Designing a product that functions properly when produced in mass is vastly more difficult than most people realize. Even engineers and designers with decades of experience still find the process to be challenging. If you get past that hurdle, you still have to deal with regulatory and compliance regulations that can be equally stifling. This chapter outlines the entire process of bringing your product to life so you know what you're up against and where to find the resources to make it happen.

7.1: DEFINING THE REQUIREMENTS OF YOUR PRODUCT

The first step toward developing a product is defining exactly what you want it to be. In the product development industry this is typically done with a Product Requirement Document, also known as a PRD. This document defines the necessary features and specifications of a product, acting as a blueprint for the product development team to design around. The PRD should be driven by values, priorities, and needs of your target customer. This document is especially crucial if you plan to outsource the product development process.

A comprehensive PRD should include the following:

Target customer demographic and psychographic information (Demographics: Age, Sex, Profession, etc. Psychographics: Hobbies, values, lifestyles, etc.)

Intended use (Ex. Intended to clean lint, dust, and hair off surfaces without leaving residue or damaging the surface)

Functional product requirements (Ex. Must shoot foam darts 30-40 feet)

Feature specifications (Ex. Handle should include a bottle opener)

Technical specifications (Ex. 2 liter volume, 120 grams or less total product weight)

Other requirements (Ex. Product must be made from at least 50% post-consumer recycled plastic)

Target COGS

Target MSRP

A qualified product designer should be able to use a well-developed PRD to start and guide the development of the product. Building a comprehensive PRD is one of the most important steps to ensure you get the product you want as you go through the design process. Designers and engineers are not mind readers, so if you want something to be included in your product then be sure to include it in the PRD.

7.2: PRODUCT DESIGN AND ENGINEERING:

Since you're reading this book, there's a good chance that you're an experienced engineer or designer and you want to launch your own idea. If that's the case and you have extensive knowledge and experience bringing products to life, feel free to skip ahead a few paragraphs. If you don't have a decade of experience, the next six paragraphs are for you.

An experienced product engineer or engineering consultancy should be able to help you design a functional, manufacturable product. Note that I specifically call for an "experienced" engineer. A recent college graduate with a degree in mechanical engineering will not do! They don't teach the necessary skillsets in college. The only way to gain the knowledge necessary to effectively and efficiently bring a product to market is through real-world industry experience. When you're looking for an engineer or engineering firm to help develop your product, ask to see their portfolio of work. They should have documentation of their past projects and all the different products they've helped bring to market. If they can't or won't show you their prior work, run! Interview different firms until you find one who has a proven track record of developing mass produced products that are similar to your idea. If your product includes batteries and electronics, make sure your engineering firm has successfully developed products with batteries and electronics in the past. Different types of products require different types of experience and expertise. Do your homework to ensure the engineer or engineering firm you choose has the necessary experience for your product idea.

Simply having your product engineered to function and be manufacturable may not be enough. You also want it to look and feel great, right? Isn't it nice when a product fits in your hand just right and has all the buttons in the perfect place? That's what Industrial Designers do. They work alongside the engineers to ensure your product is as beautiful, usable, and ergonomic as it is functional. Industrial design services are typically not included with engineering services, so this is another expensive facet of bringing an amazing product to life. Industrial design is another profession that requires many years of experience to master, so you really don't want to cut corners here either. You should vet any prospective industrial designers or design firms with the same diligence and process as the engineering firms.

Some firms may have both engineers and designers on staff so they can deliver a beautiful and functional product to their clients with minimal hassle. If you aren't intimately familiar with the design and engineering processes, these combined firms may be a good way forward for you. There are also agencies that will take your idea and engineer it, design it, source the manufacturing, test, troubleshoot, refine, and deliver a completed product. These businesses will often have a significant upfront fee plus they mark up every unit you buy in the future. You end up paying them for the entire lifespan of the product. This may amount to a large sum of money over the life of the product, but they also provided a lot of value so they earned it. If you don't have any experience bringing a product to market, this is probably the best option for you.

Throughout the product development process you should receive incremental updates in the form of renderings, appearance models, and functional prototypes. Renderings are computer generated images that show exactly what your finished product will look like. Industrial Designers used to generate these by hand, but today they're typically done using various pieces of computer software to achieve the most realistic results. Renderings should help you dial in the aesthetic design, color, finish texture, and any other ornamental aspects of your product. Some firms will produce a physical appearance model that is a non-functional replica of your finished product so you know exactly what your product will look and feel like in the real world. Appearance models can be extremely expensive and may not be necessary for your project. At the same time, the engineering department should deliver functional prototypes throughout the process. These will often consist of 3D printed components, CNC machined parts, and prototype circuit boards. These iterative prototypes may not look exactly like the final product, but the point is to test and prove the design of the various systems along the way. At the end of the project, you'll want the industrial design and engineering teams to work together to produce a final prototype. While the colors and finishes may not all be correct, this prototype should utilize similar materials to the final design and incorporate all functional systems into the final aesthetic design of the product. You will use this final prototype to confirm that the product is everything you hoped it would be. I recommend that you don't proceed to production tooling without first building and thoroughly testing a final prototype.

It can be extremely difficult to bring a quality product to market if you don't have the proper experience. One way around this issue for many entrepreneurs is to bring on a partner with the technical skillset they lack. Many of us know a few brilliant engineers or designers and their knowledge and experience could be the difference in stalling out vs. getting the product over the finish line. If you have little experience in the product world, I'd strongly suggest that you consider finding a technical partner to round out your skillset.

Engineering and design are a pair of topics that could easily fill an entire bookshelf, so we won't be doing much more than scratching the surface for the purposes of this book. The big takeaway should be that the process of preparing a product for mass production is quite difficult and requires a lot of experience and expertise. If you don't have this experience and expertise you should partner with someone who does, whether it's a consulting firm, a design and manufacturing agency, or a business partner with a technical skillset. If you find yourself in the situation of needing help and don't know where to start looking, Kickstarter has compiled some great resources for design, engineering, prototyping, and manufacturing on their website: https://www.kickstarter.com/help/resources This list is a great place to start your search for quality service providers, whether you use the funding platform or not.

7.3: PACKAGING DESIGN CONSIDERATIONS

As you're designing your product, you should also be designing the packaging. Properly designed packaging should achieve a number of key objectives including: Protecting the product in transit, enabling proper display and merchandising at retail, displaying required regulatory information and logistical assets like barcodes and SKU numbers, keeping separate parts together, reducing opportunity for theft, enabling efficient freight, and minimizing environmental impact.

Packaging is a critical aspect of every product because of the important role it plays in safely getting the product to the consumer and attracting potential customers in the store. Your packaging should be designed to protect the product from drops, crushing, and potentially other hazards like water, dust, and stains. It also needs to look great on store shelves and clearly showcase the key features and benefits that your product offers. At the same time, you don't want to spend too much money on the packaging because it's typically discarded immediately after purchase. You should also work to minimize the environmental impact of these disposable components by reducing material consumption as much as possible and selecting compostable or recyclable options whenever you can. This is important to many consumers and most retailers, so it's good for both business and the environment.

You also want to ensure your packaged product doesn't occupy more space than necessary to achieve all these objectives. Shipping bulky products is expensive, so saving space through efficient packaging will save you money in the long run. Additionally, it can be difficult to convince a store to carry a bulky, poorly packaged product. Stores like to utilize every square inch of shelf space to offer the best possible selection to their customers. If your product wastes space in their store, they may choose not to carry it for that reason alone.

Designing good packaging is both an art and a science. Packaging design is its own profession, and it may be worthwhile for you to outsource this task if you don't feel that you're up to doing it yourself. Defective packaging can be just as troublesome as defective product, so you want to ensure this part of the project gets the attention it deserves. A quick web search for "packaging design firm" should bring up some options for you to choose from if you decide to outsource this part of the project. Your engineering or design firm may also offer packaging design services for an additional fee.

7.4: REGULATORY REQUIREMENTS AND PRODUCT CERTIFICATIONS:

In addition to design and engineering for mass production, you need to ensure your finished product will comply with the regulatory requirements of the various countries into which you intend to import. These requirements are different for different types of products and it will require some research to determine what is necessary. At minimum, the product will need to list the country of manufacture. This is why so many products have "Made in China" stamped on them. Many products have additional requirements beyond that. For example, fabric products should list the fabric composition (ex. 80% nylon, 20% polyester) and the care and washing instructions (Ex. machine wash cold, tumble dry low). If you have plans to sell internationally, you also need to list these stats in a number of languages including English, French, Spanish, German, Italian, Dutch, and Japanese. These languages will cover most of the countries that require local language for import.

If you're making a product that will contact food, you need to ensure that the materials you use are food-safe. It's common practice to ensure your food-safe products are BPA and PVC free as well. This will require lab testing from a qualified test lab like SGS, Intertek, or UL.

If your product has batteries, electronics, or transmits signals, additional certifications will be required. FCC certifications are required on the vast majority of electronic products. UL certifications are required in the U.S. and Canada for products that plug in to an AC outlet, and a similar CE certification is required across Europe. If you are making a toy, there is a whole litany of requirements and restrictions you must follow as outlined in a document called ASTM F963-17. You also have California Proposition 65 to contend with, regardless of your product category. If your product contains any of the chemicals on the list published here: https://oehha.ca.gov/proposition-65/proposition-65-list then you must label your product according to the requirements of CA Prop65 if you intend to sell in the State of California.

Don't underestimate the time and resources required to ensure your product is compliant and properly certified. Depending on your product this testing can take a couple of weeks or many months to complete. It can also be a great expense for certain categories of product. Do your homework up front and consider asking your engineering firm to help you through the process if you aren't comfortable going it alone.

7.5: PATENTS

There are two primary types of patents that you should be aware of: Utility patents and design patents. Utility patents are intended to protect the way an invention is used and/or functions. This is what people are most commonly referring to when they speak of "patents" broadly. Design patents are intended to protect the way an item looks. These are useful in preventing someone else from making a product that looks exactly like your product. Nearly any product can receive a design patent, but that's only useful if you're worried about protecting the ornamental design of your invention. Utility patents are a bit more difficult to obtain and these are what we'll be focusing on throughout the rest of this section. Before we continue, this seems like another great place to mention that I'm not a patent attorney and nothing in the book should constitute legal advice. The information here is a reflection of my personal experience with patents and the patent process as an experienced product entrepreneur. Patent attorneys will have a very different viewpoint on these topics, but they also have different incentives and priorities than the product entrepreneur.

Patents are often a major sticking point for aspiring product entrepreneurs, but I encourage you not to get too hung up on them. A patent does not validate your idea and it doesn't ensure it will work or be profitable. There are thousands of terrible ideas and worthless concepts patented every month. Unless your goal is to sell your patent to another company, the reality is that your patent is only as good as the resources you have to enforce it. If a major corporation infringes on your patent, will you have the time and money necessary to sue them and recover your losses? That process will most likely take years and millions of dollars to resolve. It's generally reported that the average cost of patent litigation is far north of 1.5 million dollars. If you don't think you'll have a couple million dollars lying around to spend on a patent suit in the near future, is having a patent really going to be that beneficial for you? In addition to being expensive and difficult to enforce, patents are typically pretty easy to work around. With so much existing technology and so many pre-existing patents (collectively referred to as "prior art" in the patent world), it's pretty rare to come up with a totally new idea that will receive a broad enough patent to provide a useful level of protection for your invention. Most modern patents are pretty narrow, and clever engineers can often skirt around your claims to make a product that does the exact same thing without infringing on your patent. This is a bummer, but it's also reality.

There are certain ideas that do warrant a patent. If you've invented an important or valuable new technology that has massive potential for success, I encourage you to pursue a strong utility patent. If your invention is extremely simple and could easily be covered with a couple of core claims, a patent may also be of value to you. Simpler and more novel devices are often easier to patent, more difficult to copy without infringement, and can be slightly cheaper to enforce or litigate. You will need to hire a qualified patent attorney to write and file your utility patent. The cost for this typically starts around $4,000 on the low side and goes up from there.

There is another great patent option that I highly recommend and use often myself; the provisional patent. A provisional patent is not actually a patent, but it does establish an early filing date that you can use for your non-provisional patent in the future. The non-provisional patent must be filed within 1 year of the provisional patent filing date. This 1-year period gives you the time necessary to evaluate the commercial potential of your idea while still reserving your ability to patent the invention with the provisional patent's priority date. This can be a great tool if you want to see how your product sells before you spend the money to file a utility patent, or if you want to shop your idea around to potential investors while mitigating the risk that they copy your idea and launch it themselves.

A provisional patent can be written and filed by the entrepreneur and costs less than $150 for most small businesses (even less for "micro-entities"). You need to fully document your invention using photos, drawings, and detailed written descriptions. Try to cover any future "claims" you might want to make on your non-provisional patent in excruciating detail. Include any potential alternative designs you can think of as well. Then put this all together with a completed cover sheet from the USPTO, include payment, and mail it in. You can find detailed instructions for filing a provisional patent on the USPTO.gov website.

7.6: MANUFACTURING OPTIONS; CONTRACT MANUFACTURING VS. DIY MANUFACTURING

After your product has been designed, you need to figure out how you're going to get it manufactured. You generally have two options for manufacturing: you can do it yourself or use a contract manufacturer. Depending on the product, your experience, and a number of other factors, either may be appropriate. However, there are some very compelling reasons to choose one over the other.

DIY manufacturing requires you to hire employees, buy machinery, set up a factory, and manage the entire operation daily. This method can be effective for launching a product, though your ability to grow will be limited by your ability to expand operations and produce higher volumes. There are a lot of benefits of manufacturing your own products: better margins, less inventory needed, more control over quality, etc. However, there are also a lot of downsides; mainly that you have to invest in, and manage a factory in addition to the rest of your business! Trust me when I say that you will have plenty on your plate as it is. Unless manufacturing is your background or your product is incredibly simple to produce, your time is probably better spent on growing your business, not managing the day-to-day operations of a factory.

As a disclaimer, I have seen product businesses launch and grow into very successful, multi-million dollar operations while doing their own manufacturing. These businesses were all started by people who have decades of experience running a factory so they leverage this experience to beat out the competitors. If you aren't an experienced manufacturing expert with the resources to build and manage a manufacturing facility, I recommend a different route; contract manufacturing.

A contract manufacturer is a factory you pay to produce your product for you. They should manage all the operations inside their own facility. They are responsible for buying new machinery, machine maintenance, employing and training workers, etc. Your concern becomes the price, lead time, and quality of the end product. Contract manufacturing allows you to get your product to market quickly and efficiently because you don't have to set all that up. You also don't have to pay for it all upfront and you get to leverage the expertise of the staff and management of that factory.

Contract manufacturing also enables you to expand your production capabilities quickly when your product becomes a raging success. You do expect your product to be a huge success, right? Consider this scenario: You've been selling your product successfully online and through a few hundred smaller retailers for around two years. You're selling around 5000 units per month. Then you get a meeting with Wal-Mart and your product has caught their attention. They want it in every store nationwide. You undergo the vendor setup process and finally get that first purchase order. Maybe you didn't realize exactly what quantities "every store" would translate to for a store like Wal-Mart. They want to load-in over 4700 stores with 6 units at each store. That's an initial order of over 28,000 units. Then they expect to sell 2 units per store per week. Sounds manageable, right? That's nearly 38,000 units per month! That doesn't even include the 5,000 per month you were already selling. You need to scale up fast.

Hopefully you thought through the numbers when you got the inquiry from Wal-Mart and you gave your contract manufacturer a call. They were either thrilled or they told you that they wouldn't be able to handle the volume. If they're thrilled and they can handle it, that's fantastic. If they can't and you're already used to working with contract manufacturers, you can always bring on a second factory to help with the extra demand.

With contract manufacturing the cost of the equipment, maintenance, heating and cooling the factory building, paying worker salaries, costly mistakes, accidents, etc. are all rolled into the quoted price of your product. It's their job to figure all that out and manage it. Unless running a factory is your expertise, I recommend steering clear of it. Keep your operations simple whenever you can.

Contract manufacturing isn't all rainbows and butterflies, though. There are just as many downsides as upsides. Your margins aren't as good, you have less direct control over quality and lead times, you will have to carry more inventory of each SKU, and you're not always their top priority. On the upside, you don't have to invest in an entire factory to get started. You don't have to run the entire manufacturing operation, and you don't have to undergo the very long and steep learning curve of learning to manage a factory.

7.7: SOURCING AND SELECTING A CONTRACT MANUFACTURER

If you've decided against manufacturing your own products, it's time to find a contract manufacturer that suits your needs. This is where so many aspiring product entrepreneurs seem to stall out, but it's really not that difficult. Let's walk through the process.

First, consider where in the world you should manufacture your product. Most things are made in China these days but that's not always the right answer. Contrary to common assumption, it can be cost effective to manufacture certain products in the U.S. or other developed countries. The cost of materials is somewhat similar across the globe but the cost of labor varies greatly. So, if your product requires very little labor to produce then you may able to manufacture it locally for a competitive rate. This is especially true with low-labor, bulky items that are expensive to ship. A few examples of products that meet this criteria would be kayaks, coolers, and car tires. Most products will not meet this criteria, especially if there's a significant amount of labor required to produce or assemble the product. This is when overseas production starts to make sense.

When you manufacture overseas you'll have to contend with import duties and freight costs. Import duties are tariffs paid to the federal government when you import certain items from certain countries. Every item category has a different duty rate and it often varies by the country of origin as well. You'll want to do a little research on the import duty rates of your product when you're deciding where to place your manufacturing. You might find that a product with 42.6% duties from China can be imported from Cambodia at 0%. A little research might save you nearly 50% on your COGS! You can find duty rates for every product category on the Customs and Border Patrol website at CBP.gov, but the process is not simple. You may need to ask a qualified freight forwarder to assist with classification. We touch on this more in chapter 8.

In addition to duty rates, some countries are better-known for manufacturing certain items than others. Vietnam is famous for making high-quality sewn goods and Taiwan is well-known for electronics, for example. It's worth your time to do a little research on which countries specialize in your product type because these specialties are often more than just a stereotype. You want to ensure your factory has access to an adequate supply of trained operators, raw materials, knowledgeable engineers, experienced factory managers, and the proper equipment to manufacture your product. All places are not equal in the world of manufacturing.

In some instances there won't be an obvious choice for country of manufacture. When this happens, it's often easiest to default to China. There are competent manufacturers in China across virtually every product category, and they're easier to find in China than anywhere else. The sheer number of options and relative ease of sourcing in China are the reasons it has become the default choice for so many product companies.

Now that you've narrowed down where you want to manufacture, you need to pinpoint a specific factory for the job. It's important to realize that every manufacturer has their specialty. This may be injection molding, metal fabrication, CNC machining, sewing, circuit board manufacturing, assembly, or something else. Virtually no factory can do all these things well. So, if you have a complex product idea that utilizes a number of materials or manufacturing processes, you might need to work with multiple component manufacturers. You then send all those individual parts to an assembly house for final assembly and packaging. If this doesn't sound like a realistic feat, you can often quote your entire product at the factory that will make the majority of the components and they will take the liberty of outsourcing all of the parts they can't make themselves (at a markup of course!).

There are a few key resources for finding quality overseas factories. The best of these resources are sourcing fairs. These are essentially tradeshows where manufacturers from different industries come together under a single roof to show off their capabilities. The crème de la crème of sourcing fairs is the Canton Fair that happens twice per year in Guangdong, China. You need to do your research and planning well in advance because there are three sessions that each contain different product categories. Each session hosts thousands of factories who are excited to take on new business. They bring examples of products they manufacture so you can get an idea of their product quality and capabilities immediately. If you plan to source product in China, I strongly encourage you to attend the Canton Fair to find your future supplier. Many other countries host similar sourcing fairs at a smaller scale as well.

If you don't have the resources or opportunity to attend a sourcing fair where you plan to manufacture, there are still some great domestic options. Industry tradeshows will often have an "international" section where international manufacturers exhibit their capabilities to attract new business. One example of this type of show is the Outdoor Retailer tradeshow that is held twice annually in Denver, CO. The bottom floor hosts a few hundred manufacturers from all over the world and you can speak to them in person without ever leaving the country.

You can also source manufacturers online from the comfort of your couch, though it's a bit more challenging. ImportGenius. com is a great resource to see what manufacturers other companies are using to make their products. Simply go to the website and enter the name of a U.S. company that makes similar products to yours. Import Genius will show you the names of their top international trading partners. This information is compiled from U.S. Customs records so it's typically pretty reliable. Once you know the factory names, you can often find their website and, subsequently, their contact information. This can be a great starting point for finding a qualified factory.

Alibaba.com is another great resource for finding factories throughout China and even in some other countries. It's really intended for sourcing OEM components, but most factories listing on Alibaba are happy to accept new projects. You should begin by searching Alibaba for products similar to your own. This will hopefully give you a bunch of listings of similar products, including the contact information for the factory who makes them. Reach out to several potential manufacturers through the Alibaba messenger and see who eagerly gets back to you. Keep in mind that they're probably in a vastly different time zone so they may not message you back immediately. One great thing about Alibaba is their Trade Assurance program. If you pay for your product through Alibaba, you are financially covered if the factory fails to deliver your product or does not meet the quality specification in the production contract. This is a free service Alibaba provides to create trust between the buyer and supplier.

You'll probably receive messages back from a number of prospective suppliers, so you need to start narrowing them down. First and foremost, try to move forward with factories that seem eager to have your business. If they are too busy to give you attention during the courting process, you will be a low priority for them once you are a customer as well. Second, look for fast and clear communication. The language barrier can be difficult to overcome so having someone with whom you can communicate clearly is important. Third, try to ensure they know their stuff! If you send CAD files and they can't figure out what program to use to open the file, they probably aren't a good fit. They should be technically proficient in their craft. Fourth, the price quote should be competitive. I encourage you to go with the factory you feel best about rather than the cheapest, because you will often pay dearly for choosing the cheapest option. However, they should be competitive with the other options. To get a quote you will need to send over detailed design documentation, drawings, CAD files, assembly instructions, etc. If you aren't familiar with these documents, your design and engineering firms should be able to deliver the documentation you need.

Another important aspect of sourcing internationally is ensuring that your prospective factories adhere to human rights and environmental regulations, as well as any personal expectations that you may have on these topics. You should ask prospective factories for any third-party certifications they have regarding human rights and environmental policy. Many factories have paid for independent third parties to evaluate their business practices, certifying that they pay their people a living wage, mitigate workplace hazards, and manufacture in a way that does not do excess harm to the environment. This isn't just something you should do for your own conscience; it's also a very smart business practice. Factories are frequently shut down for environmental and human rights violations and you don't want to see your factory get shuttered. A disruption of this magnitude could ruin your business. Additionally, many major retailers require factory audits or certifications before they will put your product on their shelves. You don't want to miss an opportunity with a major retailer because you didn't do your due diligence when selecting your factory.

If all this is feeling a bit overwhelming, there is another option; you can use a sourcing agent. Sourcing agents will take your design and find you a qualified manufacturer. You typically place your orders directly with the agent and they pass the order on to the factory. They will, of course, apply a markup for their services. You pay a little more for every product but they do all the work of finding, vetting, and managing the manufacturers. Agents can also handle the logistics of getting the product all the way to you warehouse. They should be able to give you a single "landed" price quote that includes freight to your destination and import duties. This can be a very appealing and effective option, especially for new product entrepreneurs. The experience of a good sourcing agent may save you a lot of heartache and money if you don't know what you're doing in the sourcing world. If you're interested in using a sourcing agent for your manufacturing, a quick web search should produce some good options to get you started. Agents typically work pretty hard to make themselves visible to those who are searching for them online.

If you decided to use a consulting firm for your design and engineering needs, they might also be able to help with sourcing. Many firms provide this service as a value-add to their customers. This can often be done without impacting the final product cost since you're paying for their services up-front.

As you progress in your factory search, you really want to do as much as possible to understand the level of service they will provide in the future. Don't hesitate to request some sample parts that they've made in the past so you can evaluate the quality. You can also ask for references or inquire about other companies for whom they manufacture. It's a good sign if they manufacture for some quality brands that you're familiar with. Check to see if they have any status badges on Alibaba.com like "gold supplier" status. If possible, arrange a visit to your prospective factories before you commit to working with them. Try to set up a meeting with the owner and your future account manager so you can all put faces to name. These small steps may seem trivial but they're very important in selecting a good manufacturing partner.

7.8: PRICE QUOTES, BILL OF MATERIALS, AND INCOTERMS

Once you have the field narrowed to just a few potential suppliers, it's time to get a price quote on your product. If your product is novel, contains potential intellectual property, or if you're worried someone may copy or steal your idea, it is wise to have prospective factories sign a non-disclosure agreement (NDA) before you send your design. You can have an attorney create an NDA for you, or you can find a free NDA template or an NDA creator online that will do an adequate job for most situations. After the NDA is signed by the prospective factory, send your design documentation and request a price quote. The quote should separately itemize the upfront cost for any required tooling (injection molds, stamping tools, assembly jigs, etc.) and the individual unit cost. This quote will typically include the minimum order quantity (MOQ) and any applicable price breaks for ordering in higher quantities. I recommend always quoting at least 3 suppliers on any project because pricing can vary significantly.

Alongside the basic quote showing the tooling and piece-part cost for your project, you may want to request a Bill of Materials, or BOM. A BOM contains an itemized list of every component the manufacturer will produce and lists the corresponding price. The BOM should list labor as a separate line item. In addition to just being good practice, having this document can be extremely helpful in any cost reduction exercises you may need to do on your product. It's not uncommon for one or two unique components to vastly drive up the cost of an entire product. You might be able to change that one expensive component from metal to plastic, for example, and cut the cost by a factor of 10. These are things you will only be able to explore if you have a full BOM for your product.

As you're getting price quotes, it's important that you understand the incoterms being used for the quoted price. "Incoterms" stands for "International Commercial Terms" and this is basically a set of globally-accepted commercial terms of sale. Most factories will provide their quote using "FOB" terms, which stands for "Free on Board." FOB typically means that the factory will cover the expense of taking the goods to port and loading them on a ship. The ownership transfers from the seller to the buyer after the goods are loaded. All remaining expenses including freight, duties, and unloading are the buyer's responsibility. FOB terms are extremely common and work well for most applications. EXW and DDP are other commonly used incoterms. EXW stands for EX Works, which means that the seller only has to make the finished goods available at their factory. This does not include freight to the local port or loading on the ship. DDP stands for Delivered Duty Paid and these terms place a lot of responsibility on the factory. With DDP Terms, the factory or seller must deliver the goods all the way to the specified destination (usually your warehouse) for the specified price. This price must include all freight and import duties. DDP terms make life very easy for the buyer because the selling factory has to handle all the logistics. As with everything, you can expect to pay a markup on the freight and duties if you request DDP terms.

You can request specific incoterms when you request your quote. You should expect to get slightly better per-unit pricing if you request EXW terms than FOB, and you should expect significantly lower pricing with FOB terms than DDP. Keep in mind that you'll still incur some expense in getting the product to port and loading it on a ship if you choose EXW terms.

Your quote should also include payment terms. Typical payment terms for factories require an initial deposit to start production and a balance payment upon completion of the order. A 50% deposit, 50% balance payment structure is a fairly common arrangement. 30/70 is not uncommon for companies with a good payment history. There will typically be a similar payment structure for any tooling required to produce your product. You may be required to pay for 50% of the tooling cost up front and 50% after the tooling is built and fully functional. Pay close attention to the payment terms on your quote because this will impact your cash flow in the future.

7.9: DFM REPORTS (DESIGN FOR MANUFACTURING)

After you receive your quote, the next step is to request a DFM report from the factory. DFM stands for Design for Manufacturing, and the corresponding report should outline the details of the manufacturing process and any issues the factory foresees with manufacturing your design. If your product includes injection molded parts, the DFM report should show the basic tooling structure including the location of witness lines, ejector pins, gates, sprues, etc. It should also indicate areas where you don't have enough draft on your parts, or where there could be mold-fill issues. The report will be a bit different for every manufacturing process, but a good factory should be able to send a comprehensive DFM report on every part of your product.

There's a good chance that some minor design changes will be required after you receive the DFM report. This is quite common and it's typically a result of the limitations of certain mass production processes, or the equipment a specific factory has available. Try to be as accommodating to these requested changes as you reasonably can because pushing back or refusing to make the changes will often result in a high defect rate during production. If you make design tweaks to accommodate the requests in the DFM report, be sure to build a complete prototype with these recent changes implemented before you start the tooling process. Even minor design changes can produce unintended results, so you always want to verify your complete design with a fully functional prototype before you move forward with expensive tooling. If you have outsourced your design and engineering processes, the consulting firms should be able to manage the DFM process and provide the necessary feedback on your behalf.

7.10: PLACING YOUR FIRST PRODUCTION ORDER

The big moment is finally here! You're ready to place the first order of your very own product! Before you do though, you should strongly consider putting a manufacturing contract in place between you and your chosen factory. This contract should outline the key specifications of the product, quality control requirements, and what happens if these requirements aren't met. Hopefully you'll never need this agreement, but it's great to have when things go sideways.

To formally place an order with the factory you need to first email them a purchase order, commonly called a PO. Your PO should include the name and description of the item, the material, the quantity you intend to purchase, the price, as well as your company info, date, and an identifying PO number. You can download a PO template online or, better yet, generate a custom PO using your accounting software. The factory will receive the PO and reply with a Pro Forma Invoice, also called a PI. The PI is basically a preliminary invoice for the goods they intend to sell you. It should include similar information to the PO plus the incoterms and payment terms to be used in the transaction. To finalize the order simply sign the PI and email it back to the factory. The signed PI should be accompanied by the deposit payment to get the project rolling.

7.11: PAYING INTERNATIONAL SUPPLIERS

Now that you've signed the PI, you need to pay the deposit. The factory typically won't start working on your product until the deposit has been received. If your factory is based in the same country as you, paying is as easy as mailing a check or initiating an ACH transfer through your online banking portal. This is also the case if you're working with a sourcing agent based in your home country. However, it's a bit more difficult to pay an international supplier.

There are a few common ways to send money overseas. The most frequent method is called a wire transfer. Wire transfers are very quick, cannot be reversed, and typically cost around $45 each to send and $15 or more to receive. These are great for sending large lump sums of money where the $60 in bank processing fees is a negligible percentage. PayPal is another common method for sending funds overseas but is better used for smaller transactions since the fees are based on a percentage of the total sent. There is another service I like to use to pay suppliers called Veem. This is a financial service similar to PayPal that specializes in international money transfers with reduced fees.

Be very careful to avoid fraud when sending a wire transfer to a new supplier. It is an extremely common scam for an unknown third party to send incorrect bank information to a buyer right before the transaction so that the money is directed to the wrong bank account. Due to the prevalence and severity of this scam, I recommend requesting the banking information for any new supplier in person or on a video call where you can see your supplier's face. This is the only way to ensure you get the proper bank account information for your wire transfer.

7.12: PRE-PRODUCTION SAMPLES AND SAMPLE TESTING

Now that you've placed the initial order and paid the deposit, it's time for your factory to get to work. They should start building the necessary tooling and ordering the raw materials to mass produce your product. This process can take some time, varying from a few weeks to many months depending on the complexity of your product. Make a habit of requesting a status update at least every two weeks so you stay aware of any major setbacks or delays.

Once the factory has completed their first pass at the tooling for your product, they should make you some pre-production samples using these new mass production tools. It's important to understand that everything may not fit and function perfectly on the first try. It takes some trial and error to dial in mass production tooling to get the perfect fit and finish on every part. If you're using a consulting firm for your product development process, you can have the samples sent directly to them so they can provide feedback on fit, finish, and function. The process of dialing in your tooling for mass production may seem insignificant, but it's often the primary differentiator between high-end and low-quality products.

Once you have functional pre-production samples, you can start testing. Testing may include laboratory testing, function testing, durability testing, and specification testing. Laboratory testing may include the certification processes mentioned earlier in this chapter. Function testing should involve you and potentially a select group of trusted beta-testers using the product to find any potential functional issues before you bring the product to market. Durability testing should include vigorous real-world use testing as well as any applicable torture testing that should be done in a laboratory setting, like a drop test. Specification testing can also involve real-world or lab testing, but should be done to verify that the product meets all the claimed specifications. A good example of this would be waterproof ratings. You may need to do some independent lab testing to verify that your product can withstand water pressure of a certain depth for a certain time (this is called an IP rating). Some tests can be performed by the entrepreneur directly, while others should be done by an independent test lab.

It's important that you don't take any shortcuts on your testing process. You've spent too much time and money getting to this point to fall short on testing. Consider the ramifications of not catching a critical product issue before you manufacture the item in mass quantities. You will have all your money tied up in a big batch of unsellable, defective product. This is a terrible situation that can often be avoided by thoroughly and extensively testing your product before you start mass production.

7.13: MANAGING FACTORY TIMELINES

After all the testing is complete and all the kinks are worked out with your production tooling, you can officially kick off mass production on your first batch of product. At this point, you may feel like the ball is fully in the factory's court so you can sit by and wait on them to finish. While that's how it should go, that's definitely not how it does go. Factories are dealing with a number of different customers, a lot of raw material suppliers, sub-contractors, employees, and dozens of other complex moving parts. If you aren't checking in constantly on the status of your order, you may find that the factory will slip on deadlines without letting you know. I once had a production run slip by more than 90 days because I failed to check in regularly. The expected ship date came and went. I inquired with the factory to find out that they hadn't even started production yet!

To avoid this situation, I strongly encourage you to send a weekly check-in email to your factory requesting a status update and the current estimated completion date of your project. This small task will keep you abreast of any potential delays, keep your project on top of mind for the factory, and even circumvent some delays. It's not uncommon for an entire production run to be delayed because a single component is late. I've seen something as small as a specific model number of a plastic buckle on a backpack cause massive delays. If you're aware of the delay and the underlying cause, perhaps you can substitute that buckle for another model and avoid a long delay. This is only possible if you stay up to date on your projects and maintain constant communication with your factory.

7.14: BEING A GOOD BUSINESS PARTNER; YOU GET WHAT YOU GIVE

Your contract manufacturing relationship should be seen as a long-term partnership that requires give and take. Just like you hope that your factory will treat you well and work in your best interest, you need to be an equally good partner to them in return. You should make every effort to uphold your commitments, make payments on time, and do your best to keep the project moving forward. If you can't uphold your end of the deal, you shouldn't expect them to either. Be mindful of their time and their margins. If they can't make a profit from working with you, they won't give you a high level of service. It will benefit you greatly to become your factory's favorite customer. This will get you the best possible service, the ability to ask small favors without being nickel-and-dimed, and sometimes priority in the production queue over less-preferred customers. Wouldn't you rather see somebody else's project get bumped instead of your own? If so, make efforts to become your factory's favorite customer.

Sometimes, despite everyone's best efforts, things go wrong. In these situations you should try to remember that these factories are comprised of entrepreneurs and employees who are doing their very best, just like you. Their business is difficult and mistakes happen from time to time. You might get a batch of defective product, or maybe a deadline gets missed. This is not uncommon at all in the product industry. When things go poorly, it's important to handle the issue like a professional and work together with your factory to find the best possible resolution. Always remember, the better partner you are to them, the better they will be to you in return.

When you run into issues with your factory, always take a proactive solution-centric approach. There are often ways to amicably resolve major issues while actually strengthening the relationship in the process. If your factory sees that your are keeping their interests in mind while you work to solve the problem, they will often reciprocate. The best solutions usually require some creativity and flexibility from both sides, so you want the factory on your team helping to solve the problem instead of playing the blame game and passing fault. The ability to creatively resolve problems with minimal impact is often the difference between entrepreneurs who succeed and those who fail. Try to keep this in mind as you progress in your product business.

CHAPTER 8:

LOGISTICS

Now that you've started mass production on your product, the next step in the process is figuring out how to efficiently move your product from the factory to the end consumer. This process is much more complex than it sounds and doing it well requires a lot of preparation and knowledge. Don't worry, we'll cover all those gritty details in this chapter.

To ensure your product can efficiently flow through the supply chain to the end consumer, your preparation starts with the product itself. The product must be properly labeled, packed, and protected to arrive on time and in good condition. Next, you must understand how to move the product from the factory to the country where it will be sold. This will require export and import if you're not manufacturing where you're selling. You also need to set up a facility where you can store and ship your products, so we'll talk about warehousing. Last, you need to understand how to efficiently move the products from your warehouse to your customer. There is some additional complexity when you start working with distributors and retailers, but we'll cover that in chapter 12.

8.1: SKU NUMBERS

One of the first steps in preparing your product for distribution is giving it a Stock Keeping Unit (SKU) number. This number acts as a unique identifier for you, your factory, your warehouse, your distributors, your retailers, and nearly anyone else in your supply chain who deals directly with the product. A SKU "number" is usually an alphanumeric string of numbers and letters that helps you identify an exact product in a specific size, color, and quantity. SKU numbers help to prevent miscommunications and reduce mistakes throughout the supply chain. As the brand and the originator of the product, you get to make these numbers up! There is no controlling authority who determines what number you should use or how you should formulate a SKU number. In fact, you could make up a totally random jumble of letters and numbers to use as your SKU number, but I certainly don't recommend it. Wouldn't it be great if you could identify the product in question at a glance using only the SKU number? The answer is yes – it would be great. This is especially great once you have a whole line of products that include different colors and sizes, potentially under a number of different brands.

Over the years I've formulated a system for assigning and managing SKU numbers within my own company. I recommend that you adopt a variant of this system for yourself. In my system, the SKU number starts with two or three letters that identify the brand name. The next two letters identify the product name, style, or type. The following digit or two identifies the size of the product (Example: S, M, L, or 32). The next three digits indicate the quantity in the package. For a single unit this will be 001. For a case pack of 144 units this will be 144. The last digit or two indicates the color of the item using common color abbreviations. I try to keep my SKU numbers between 8-12 characters in length. Eight characters seems to be adequate to prevent accidental overlap with other companies' products and 12 characters is often the maximum number that some systems will accept.

Let's walk through an example: Say you make handbags under the brand name "Pouche" and you plan to release a small pink clutch for the upcoming season. Using the system outlined above, we would pull some descriptive letters from the brand name – maybe "PCH" to abbreviate Pouche. Then we would use the letters "CL" to describe the style, which is a "clutch." Next we would use "S" to describe the size as Small, and 001 to describe the single unit quantity. Last, we would use "PK" to indicate that the color is pink. When you put this together you have the SKU number PCHCLS001PK. Once you're familiar with the system, you will be able to know exactly what product is being referred to from a quick glance at the SKU number.

At this point you may be wondering about the three digit quantity denotation (001 in the current example). This is used to differentiate and specify the quantity inside cartons and case boxes of the product. For example, if you have a carton of these bags shipping to a retailer, the carton will have a SKU of its own. If there are 12 units inside the carton, you would use the SKU number PCHCLS012PK. This quickly tells you that this is a carton containing 12 units of the small pink clutch. If you're shipping a master carton to a distributor and it contains 144 pieces (12 boxes of 12 units), the SKU number on the master carton will be PCHCLS144PK. Again, you know exactly the product and quantity you're shipping at a quick glance.

8.2: BARCODES

Another important product identifier that you're probably already familiar with is the barcode. Barcodes consist of a series of black lines of varying width and they're typically found on the packaging of nearly every product you see. The barcode is what the cashier scans at checkout. Scanning the barcode quickly and seamlessly identifies the product in the store's system, adds the item price to your total, and removes the product from the store's inventory system all at once. The barcode is used for speedy product identification by a number of players throughout the supply chain, including warehouses, distribution centers, and retailers. Even third-party platforms like Amazon.com use barcodes as the primary identifying feature of the products they handle.

Each barcode is linked to a unique number called the UPC (Universal Product Code). Unlike SKU numbers, you don't get to make these up and there is a central controlling agency that manages and assigns them. This controlling agency is called GS1 and their website is www.GS1.org. You don't need to shop around because GS1 is the only legitimate provider of UPCs. When you reach the point where you need a barcode to place on your product packaging, simply make an account and pay the annual fee to get access to your first 10 barcodes. These can be generated instantly in the GS1 online platform called Data Hub. You will be asked to enter some basics about the product like dimensions, weight, price, SKU number, and package quantity. You can also create a hierarchy for each product that generates specific barcodes for each inner carton and master case pack of the product. Using our prior example of the Pouche clutch, scanning the barcode on the outside of the master case pack would quickly indicate that there are 144 units of the small pink Pouche clutch inside the box.

Once you've generated the barcode for your product and the corresponding inner cartons and master cases, you'll want to make sure that every product you produce gets properly labeled with the correct barcode. The individual product barcode should be printed in an obvious location on the exterior of the product packaging. It must be easily scannable by a cashier or, in the case of master carton boxes, an automated scanning system at a distribution center. The case and carton barcodes should be clearly printed on each box containing multiple products. Having your product and all corresponding carton and case packs properly barcoded will greatly reduce mistakes throughout your distribution network and ensure that your products are ready for retail.

8.3: MASTER CASES AND INNER CARTONS

We've spent a lot of time discussing inner cartons and master cases of your product, so you may be wondering what those are and why they're necessary. Master cases are the largest box in which you make your product available for purchase. These are typically bought by distributors or major retailers who need large quantities of your product. Inner cartons come inside the master case and they also contain a distinct number of products, though fewer than a master case. A single store will often order product in an inner carton quantity.

These packages of your product serve several key functions, especially for smaller items. First and foremost, you need some container to hold your products during transit and a cardboard box works pretty well. There really aren't many alternatives unless you're shipping really large items. Second, you need to protect your product and the retail packaging during shipment, so you want something sturdy and durable for protection. A good master case box will have thick corrugated walls and a minimum edge crush rating of 200 pounds to ensure the contents don't get squished when the boxes are stacked in a cargo container. Third, having your products neatly packed in inner cartons and master cases can have some efficiency benefits. Most warehouses charge a "pick fee" on every item they ship for you. This fee covers the labor of "picking" the product off the warehouse shelf and putting it in a box for shipment. Once you're selling to retailers in multiple quantities, say 6 units of each item per store, it becomes 6 times more efficient to pick a single

6-pack of the item rather than picking 6 individual items. The same goes for master cases. If a distributor wants 144 units of your product, it will often be 144 times cheaper to pick a single master case of your product than it would be to pick 144 individual units. Individual picks typically start around $.20 and go up from there, often depending on weight and other factors. If you do the math, you'll see that the savings of using inner cartons and master cases can add up quickly. In the example of a 144 piece master carton, you may have saved as much as $28.60 on pick fees in a single shipment!

As you can probably infer from reading these examples, it's best practice to try to predict how many units a typical store will want to order and use that number for your inner carton quantity. 6 piece inner cartons are fairly typical for most products. If your product is expensive or niche (ex. camera bags or fishing reels), perhaps 3 is a better number. If your product is cheap, disposable, or moves very quickly (ex. lint rollers or toothbrushes) you may want to use an inner carton of 48 pieces or more.

For master cases, you want to try to predict how many units a distributor may want to buy at once. 6 or 12 inner cartons is typically a good place to start. One additional consideration with master cases is that you don't want to make them so big or heavy that they're difficult to handle. Boxes over 50 pounds or measuring over 105 inches in length plus girth (Length + 2x Width + 2x Height) may incur an additional surcharge with some shipping couriers.

Your product will typically be shipped from the factory in master cases that have been stacked on pallets. Pallets are wooden skids that enable product to be moved in large batches by forklift. Since your master cases are stacked upon each other on these pallets, and other pallets may be stacked on top of that, your master case boxes need to be very sturdy. The standard specification for a master case box calls for a 200 pound edge crush force or greater. Many major retailers will specifically require that your master case boxes meet this specification so your product doesn't get damaged while in their possession. This is an important specification that you will want to pass on to your factory when you are specifying the packout procedure.

Since your product is imported in master case boxes, you need to have certain markings on the outside of each box to ensure customs clearance goes smoothly. You should ensure each master case box has the following markings: Your company name, the product name, "Made in (insert country of manufacture here)", and include the barcode for the master case of the product. You also want to include the master case SKU, the individual item SKU, the individual item name, the total quantity inside the box, the gross weight (total weight), the net weight (weight of just the sellable product), and the dimensions of the case box. By including all this information on the outside of the master case box you can ensure that everyone in the supply chain, including customs and border patrol, has all the information they need to move your master cases smoothly around the world.

Inner cartons should be labeled in a similar way with a few omissions. Markings on the inner carton boxes should include: The inner carton SKU number, item SKU number, product name, quantity in the box, "Made in (insert country of manufacture here)", and the inner carton barcode.

Note that you may not need to use inner cartons or master cases if your product is large. Under these circumstances, you might opt to put a few units or even one single unit on a wooden pallet instead. If you sell your products by the pallet, there are specific barcodes that should be created within GS1 to properly mark your pallet.

8.4: OTHER PACKOUT CONSIDERATIONS: POLYBAGS, SILICA PACKETS, ETC.

There are a few other product-level preparations that you should consider to minimize the risk of damage to your product in transit and storage. The first, and likely most controversial, is polybags. Polybags are the thin, clear plastic bags that so many products are shipped in. Even products that ship in boxes often have polybags around the product inside the box or around the outside of the box itself, and sometimes both. Polybags are controversial because they seem wasteful and they are difficult to recycle. Single-use plastics have fallen out of favor with many consumers and even some major retailers. At the same time, polybags can play a very important role in protecting your product from damage on conveyors, damage from moisture, mold, dust, contamination, and even scratches on the product or packaging. Depending on the size and type of your product, one unit ruined from not being polybagged could offset the environmental benefit and cost savings of tens-of-thousands of polybags. Polybags made of recycled content are now available and may be a good compromise until a better solution comes about.

Many retailers will require you to polybag your products before you send them to their distribution center. They don't want your product getting damaged en route to the end customer because they would be financially liable for it. If you choose to use polybags you must ensure that the barcode on the product packaging can be easily scanned through the polybag. If you make apparel and put your barcode on a paper hangtag, you must ensure that the hangtag if flipped so that the barcode can be scanned without removing the item from the polybag.

There are a few other considerations when selecting a polybag for your product. Polybags should be at least 1.5 mil (thousands of an inch) thick to ensure proper durability. They must be transparent to enable barcode scanning and easy product identification. Polybags with an opening larger than 5 inches when measured lying flat must have a child safety suffocation warning printed on the bag in large font and in a prominent location.

If your product is sensitive to moisture or might be able to harbor mold, you might want to consider using a silica packet inside your polybag to eliminate these hazards. Silica packets absorb water and moisture from the air to prevent it from damaging your product in storage. When combined with a polybag, you create a very dry, safe environment for your product that will ensure against damage through years of storage. Small silica packets often cost less than a penny, but they can be invaluable for preventing damage from condensed moisture or mold growth.

If mold growth is a major concern, you can also consider packing in a product called an O-Keep Chip alongside the silica packet. O-Keep Chips contain certain botanicals and chemicals that inhibit the growth of mold. These are commonly used to protect textiles from mold growth during shipping and storage. O-Keep Chips typically cost a few cents each.

These protections may seem like overkill but they're actually quite reasonable if you consider the conditions in which many products are packed, shipped, and stored. Many manufacturing countries are very hot, humid, and may have a lot of mold growth in and on their buildings. Mold reproduces by sending microscopic spores into the air and those can easily adhere to your product during manufacturing, assembly, and packout. Combine that with the humid air that gets trapped inside the box or polybag and you've created a great environment to grow mold on your product. Now consider that the products will get packed into a hot shipping container and shipped across the globe, potentially to somewhere quite cold. By the time they arrive, the humidity trapped inside your product's packaging has condensed and caused water damage to your product. All of this could have been prevented using proper packout techniques and materials.

8.5: FREIGHT FORWARDERS

Now that your product is properly packed and ready to ship, it's time to book your freight. If you're manufacturing in the country in which you'll be warehousing and selling, this process is quite simple. You just need to book a trucking company to pick up the product and take it to the destination. However, unless you're shipping frequently and have negotiated rates, you may find that it's actually cheaper to arrange shipment through a third party like InXpress. They have heavily negotiated discounts with trucking companies based on the volume of business they book annually. While they mark up the service a bit to sell it to you, the price with their markup included is typically much lower than non-negotiated retail rates that you'll get when you're first starting out.

The shipping process is significantly more complicated if you're manufacturing overseas because it requires export and import of your goods, customs clearance, bookings on cargo ships or planes, and freight to the final destination. Fortunately, there are freight forwarders to take care of all the details on your behalf. When you're ready to ship your product you'll contact a freight forwarder with the shipment details to get a price quote. They'll need to know the weight and dimensions of your shipment, the contents, the value, the pickup location, and the final destination. Once you confirm the quote, they'll ask for some additional information like the contact details to arrange pickup and delivery. Then they can get to work moving your goods across the world. There are a lot of freight forwarders out there, but they don't all provide the same level of service. For top-tier communication, tracking, logistics, and service, I strongly recommend looking at Flexport for your freight forwarding needs.

Freight forwarders like Flexport can arrange shipments to and from most places in the world. They can also arrange affordable shipping on a cargo ship or fast shipping on a plane. Obviously, the faster service is drastically more expensive. If you need the fastest service and the cost isn't as much of an issue, you can also use package couriers like FedEx, UPS, and DHL as your freight forwarders. They can often pick up your shipment at destination and have it in your warehouse half way around the world in just a few business days. If you plan to do this, you will definitely want to negotiate your rates with the carrier ahead of time, or ship on someone else's account who has negotiated rates and pay them back. Your factory may have great negotiated rates with a certain carrier and they will often allow you to take advantage of their rates by shipping on their account and paying back the difference.

As you're researching freight forwarders and international shipping, you'll inevitably come across some discussion on customs bonds. Customs bonds are like insurance policies for the Customs and Border Patrol office to ensure they get their duty payment for anything crossing the border. If you choose not to pay after importing goods, the company who issued the bond (called the surety) will have to pay on your behalf. Don't get too worked up about the customs bond – your forwarder will have their own and they can import your goods using their bond. However, just like with everything else, they will mark up this service. It will be cost effective to secure your own customs bond once you're importing shipments frequently. For now though, just plan to use your forwarder's custom bond.

When booking ocean shipments with your freight forwarder, you'll inevitably run across the acronyms FCL and LCL. FCL stands for "full container load" and LCL stand for "less than container load." A shipping container is one of those big metal boxes they stack on container ships, trains, and trucks. Common shipping containers are 8 feet wide, 8'6" tall, and either 20 or 40 feet long. When shipping FCL, your product will be the only product in the entire shipping container. When shipping LCL, you will share a container with products from other companies. Sharing a container is typically more cost effective if your shipment isn't large enough to fill the majority of a container, but it comes with some downsides. If the company you're sharing with fails to file the proper paperwork on time, your shipment may get delayed or scrutinized by customs since it shares a container with their product.

While the process of shipping goods internationally is quite complex, it shouldn't really be that difficult for you. A good freight forwarder will guide you through the process, assist with paperwork, and generally make the process as simple as possible. I strongly recommend using a high quality forwarder like Flexport for your first several shipments, at least until you have a good understanding of the entire process. There are cheaper couriers available, but they typically don't provide the transparency, assistance, and general service level of a premium forwarder.

8.6: DUTIES

We've talked a lot about duties in this book because they're such an important part of running a product business, especially if you choose to manufacture your product in a foreign country. Duties are the import tariffs that are assessed on a product when it is imported from a foreign country. These rates vary significantly based on the classification of the product and the country of origin (the country where the product is made).

The country of origin is usually pretty obvious and easily known. If the product is made in China, China is the country of origin. No matter where that product bounces around the world, China will always be that product's country of origin. The product's duty classification, on the other hand, is more difficult to accurately establish. You can attempt to look up your product category and establish the correct classification on the hts.usitc.gov website. However, these classifications are not always obvious and there may have been court decisions in the past that further impact classification. It's usually a good idea to have a qualified freight forwarder assist with classifying your product properly. Many forwarders will provide this as part of their service when you become a customer.

Duty classifications were harmonized worldwide in 1988 under the Harmonized Tariff System, commonly called the HTS. HTS numbers are the classification numbers used to link a product to a specific duty classification upon import, and they work across most countries. Customs will use the listed HTS number to identify the duty rate for the class of item being imported. The duties will be assessed as a percentage of the value of the shipment based on the duty rate for the item classification. The "value" of the shipment is based on your cost, not the expected resale value or the retail price. So for example, if you're importing $100,000 of backpacks from Vietnam (your cost, not retail value) and your HTS code indicates that the duty rate for this product is 17.6%, you will owe the government $17,600 to import that shipment.

8.7: WAREHOUSING AND 3PLS

To effectively run a product business you need a place to receive, store, and ship your products. Some entrepreneurs do this out of their garage and, depending on your space and time resources, this can be a valid solution in the early days of your business. I started my product business by warehousing out of a tiny house in the San Francisco Bay Area. Pallets were unloaded in the street in front of the house and I stacked boxes of inventory under the bed, along the walls, and even on the back deck under a tarp. It didn't take long before I realized that I didn't have the time or space to manage this effectively, but it was good enough to get the business off the ground with minimal expense.

If you'd like to start off with a better warehousing setup, or when you outgrow your garage, you typically have two options. Similar to the two options with manufacturing, you can either build and manage your own warehouse or you can contract someone else to do it for you. Building your own warehouse requires you to lease or buy your own space and equipment, hire staff, and manage the facility. Hiring a contract warehouse, commonly referred to as a 3PL (third party logistics company), doesn't require this level of setup or investment. It is typically more cost effective to use a 3PL until your have extremely high shipping volumes, plus you don't have to front the cost of building a warehouse or manage a warehousing operation and staff. For this reason, I typically recommend that new product entrepreneurs start off using a contract 3PL as their warehousing solution.

There are a number of 3PLs out there, from giant companies like Amazon and Ingram Micro (aka Shipwire) down to mom-and-pop warehouses that provide more customized service. The warehouse you select should be determined by your needs and their capabilities. Some warehouses specialize in apparel, which often requires custom tagging for every product that goes out the door. Others don't have the ability to do custom requests but can offer a more competitive rate for standard pick and pack services. Some 3PL companies have locations around the world so you can add distribution locations seamlessly while others may have just a single location. You will need to think through your distribution needs in detail and research the different 3PL options to find one with the service level and pricing that meets your needs.

There are a few services that should be considered non-negotiable in your search for the right 3PL. One of these is the ability to integrate their software system with your website. This is commonly called an API integration and this allows a seamless flow of information from you website to your 3PL warehouse. With an effective API integration, online orders will process and seamlessly transmit to the warehouse for shipment. Once shipped, the tracking information will be sent from the warehouse back to your website and on to the customer. This should all happen automatically and reliably, saving you a lot of time and money. Many 3PL services have pre-built apps that you can simply download and run on your website to achieve this task. If not, you might be able to use a program like ShipStation to bridge the gap between your website and the warehouse's software. However you decide to achieve the integration, I strongly urge you to only select a 3PL if this process can be automated.

If you have plans to sell your product in retail stores, your 3PL will need the ability to prepare EDI shipments. Some 3PL providers will have the ability to prepare EDI shipments themselves, while many others will only allow you to send them custom labels to apply to your EDI shipments. The former is ideal but you can get by with sending custom labels, though it is more work for you. EDI stands for "Electronic Data Interchange" and this is a system used by virtually every major retail chain to improve efficiency within their operation. We will discuss EDI in more detail in chapter 12, but for now it's important to know that your warehouse will need to have the ability to support EDI labeling requirements if you intend to sell your product at major retail stores.

As with everything else, not all 3PL providers are created equal. I've had some nightmarish experiences with various providers and others have been excellent. You should thoroughly research and potentially interview any 3PL providers you're considering working with. Try to understand the details of their pricing model, which can often be quite complex. Be sure you know the limits of their capability and the services in which they specialize. Ensure they can integrate with your website and, if you plan to sell to retail, ensure they can handle custom labeling or assist with EDI shipments. You may also want to ask whether you will have a direct contact within the actual warehouse where you store and ship your product. This can be extremely helpful when issues arise but it's actually not as common as you would think, especially with larger 3PL companies.

8.8: DOMESTIC SHIPPING CARRIERS

To get your product from the warehouse to your end customer, you'll need to use a domestic carrier like FedEx, UPS, or USPS. FedEx and UPS are fairly comparable services for most applications so you should probably use the one that gives you the deepest negotiated discount. To negotiate a discount you should call the carrier and request to be contacted by a local business account representative. That representative can work with you to evaluate your needs and negotiate a discount based on your shipping volume. Alternatively, your warehouse might have a shipping account with pre-negotiated rates that you can use instead. They can probably get deeper discounts with the carriers since their total shipping volume is the combined volume from several companies.

FedEx and UPS may provide the most reliable and economical options for many packages, but if you are shipping lightweight items, it's hard to beat the U.S. Postal Service. Domestic packages under 13 ounces and international packages under 4 pounds qualify for First Class Mail service. First Class Mail is extremely affordable, often coming in at around one-third the price of other carriers for comparable packages. The downside is that this service is less timely and less reliable, especially in high-volume times like the holidays.

Regardless of what carrier you choose to use for the majority of your shipping needs, you'll want to make an account with each of them. Business partners will often request that you ship them things on their UPS or FedEx account, and you need to have an account with the carrier to enable this capability. You should also set up a Stamps.com account so you can print USPS postage using your office printer.

By following the instructions in this chapter you should be able to efficiently and effectively move your product to the end consumer from anywhere in the world. Having the ability to deliver your product on time and in perfect condition is an absolute requirement for any successful product company. Be sure to pay attention to the details when preparing your product for transit and choosing your logistics partners. Logistical mistakes can be extremely expensive and time consuming to fix.

CHAPTER 9:

BUILDING YOUR WEBSITE

Your website should be one of your most valuable marketing tools and your highest margin sales channel. You have complete control over every aspect of your website so there's no reason it shouldn't be excellent. Your site should look great, appeal to your core customer, clearly communicate the value of your product, and allow the customer to quickly and easily buy your product and have it shipped to their doorstep. If you aren't achieving all of these objectives with your website, you're doing yourself and your brand a major disservice.

Building a website may not be your specialty, but it has actually become pretty easy to do in recent years. Don't be afraid to give it a shot. Using the tools discussed in this chapter, you can build a beautiful, functional, and scalable website with no prior experience. A few years ago, this chapter would have been a hundred pages long. Thanks to amazing advancements from some of the top web technology companies, it's now one of the simplest parts of starting your product business.

9.1: CHOOSING A REGISTRAR, HOSTING PROVIDER, AND ECOMMERCE PLATFORM FOR YOUR SITE

A domain registrar is a company that manages the registration of domain names. A hosting provider essentially gives you a location to store the data and files that make up the content of your website. The ecommerce platform provides a means of easily arranging the data and files into a beautiful and functional online store, including the cart and checkout.

Just a few years ago, these services were all segregated. You had to buy your domain name from a registrar, then subscribe to a hosting provider and add your host's DNS settings to your domain. Then you had to use the ecommerce platform to build a store on top of that. Fortunately, those days are gone. You can now register, host, and build your ecommerce store using a single service provider with minimal hassle.

As you start to research the different ecommerce platforms, you'll find that there are a lot of options: Shopify, Magento, BigCommerce, WooCommerce, Wix, Squarespace, Weebly, and dozens of others. They all have their strengths and pricing can vary quite a bit. Some are extremely easy to setup but less scalable for the future. Others are infinitely scalable but require more knowledge and expertise to setup. The one service that shines above the rest, in my opinion, is Shopify. Shopify has taken the ecommerce world by storm over the last decade due to their combination of easy setup, infinite scalability, extreme capability, and affordable plan options.

There are very few tradeoffs with the Shopify platform, so I recommend that you start and end there unless you have some very specific needs for your site.

9.2: BUILDING YOUR SHOPIFY STORE

Shopify is primarily an ecommerce platform but they also provide hosting and registrar services. This means you can buy your domain, host your site, and build your site all in one location. You don't need to understand how the back end of the internet works because they handle all of that for you, seamlessly.

After you've purchased your domain name and selected the plan that meets your needs, you're ready to select a website template. There are thousands of template options available, so you'll want to sort through them in detail to find one that works well for your needs. Some templates are designed for specific purposes – like for an apparel company with many size and color options. These templates may not work well if you only have one product to sell on your website.

You also want to make sure any template you consider is "responsive." Responsive templates are designed to change formatting when viewed on different sized devices. Now that more than half the web traffic to most stores comes from mobile phones or tablets, you can't afford to choose a template that is not responsive. Once you find a template that has the right look, function, and features, you're ready to start building!

Shopify makes building your site pretty easy. This step requires some exploration and experimentation but it's actually pretty intuitive once you get used to the interface. Most of the site building process consists of dropping in your photography, artwork, and the necessary copy to describe your product and brand. If you want to add more complexity to your site, Shopify will support that as well. The Shopify App Store has thousands of pre-built apps and plugins that will apply new capability and features to your website with a single click. If you need customization beyond that, you can always add your own custom code or hire a developer to do so. There is virtually no limit to what can be done on the Shopify platform.

As you're building your Shopify site, you may notice that product pages are built separately from the rest of the website. This is a great feature that allows you to quickly turn products on and off, categorize into collections, or update a product page without touching the rest of the website. You will create a separate product page for every different product you sell, unless they are variants of the same product. Many templates will allow you to sell size and color variations of the same product on the same product page. You may want to look for this feature when selecting a template if you plan to sell multiple sizes or colors of the same product.

While you're building your website it's important to stay true to your brand and your core customer. The language you use, the colors on your site, and the style of your photography is all very important. Refer back to your original inspiration board frequently to ensure you build a site that will really appeal to your target audience. Your website is your brand's most prominent billboard, so it's worth your time to ensure it's delivering the message you intend.

9.3: PHOTOGRAPHY AND CONTENT FOR YOUR WEBSITE

Your website will only be as good as the photography and artwork you use to build it. If you have the ability to generate top-notch photography and artwork for your website, you should absolutely do it yourself. Otherwise, it may be best to outsource this content so your website lives up to its full potential. Finding a qualified service provider for your photography or graphic design needs shouldn't be difficult. There are a number of service providers that specialize in affordable and high quality product photography for online stores and product listings. A quick web search for "product photography" will yield dozens of results for you to choose from. Fiverr.com is another great resource for the most budget conscious entrepreneurs. There you can find photographers, designers, or nearly any other type of content creator you may need for a reasonable price. 99designs.com is another affordable resource for graphic design that may yield more professional results.

You can also consider using stock photography on your website in certain scenarios. If you need a nice background image or a filler photo that elicits a certain feeling, stock photography can often be a great solution. There are many options for stock photography but Unsplash.com is my favorite. This is a totally free service that hosts high quality, rights-free photography for you to use however you like. You can search the database by keyword and download high resolution photos right from their website.

9.4: ACCEPTING PAYMENT ON YOUR WEBSITE

Shopify has a built-in payment portal called Shopify Payments that actually offers a pretty competitive processing rate. Enabling Shopify Payments on your store will instantly give your customers an easy and secure payment portal to use during checkout. You can download alternative apps to enable other service providers as well. You may find that it's best to offer a few different payment options for your customers, like Amazon Pay or PayPal. Shopify gives you the ability to install those apps through the app store, giving your customers the option to use whichever they like at checkout.

9.5: CONNECTING YOUR STORE TO YOUR WAREHOUSE

In chapter 8 we briefly discussed the ability to connect your online store to your 3PL warehouse by using an API integration. This is basically a communication link from one system to another. Because Shopify is the industry leader for online store hosting, most 3PL service providers have developed pre-built applications to link their warehousing software to any Shopify store. This will enable your online orders to seamlessly flow from your website to your warehouse. Once they are shipped, most integrations allow the tracking information to transfer back from the warehouse to your website, then transmit by email directly to your customer. With the proper setup, your orders ship and your customer receives the tracking information automatically with no work required on your behalf. Your prospective 3PL service provider should be able to tell you if they have a pre-built Shopify integration during your research phase.

9.6: CUSTOMER EMAILS: ORDER CONFIRMATION AND TRACKING

After your customer places an order, they'll expect to receive an email order confirmation and tracking information once the order ships. Shopify makes this process easy by allowing you to automate these emails through the "notifications" link on the "settings" page. You can customize the look and content of this email, and build a number of other automatically triggered emails for things like refunds, order cancellations, and more. If you're using a 3PL service for warehousing and fulfillment, you should be able to make the tracking email populate and send automatically through the API integration app with your warehouse. If you're shipping yourself, you may still have to enter the tracking information manually unless you use one of the clever shipping apps found in the Shopify app store.

9.7: WEBSITE PRIVACY POLICY AND GDPR COOKIE WARNINGS

Due to various internet-related privacy and customer tracking laws, there are a few important policies you need to add to your website to stay legal. One of these is a privacy policy. A privacy policy essentially informs website visitors of how you will gather, use, disclose, and manage their browsing data. Nearly every website you visit has one of these in place and, odds are, nobody will ever read yours. However, this doesn't mean you can skip it. Fortunately, Shopify provides a free resource to generate a customized privacy policy for your store. You can find this policy generator tool here: https://www.shopify.com/tools/policy-generator

The GDPR cookie warning is another important legal component of your website if you get any visitors from the European Union. Since you have no control over where you web visitors come from, odds are very high that you'll have a website visitor from the EU at some point. The goal of this warning is to let EU visitors know that your website collects their information through the use of cookies. There are a number of free apps in the Shopify app store that will enable a small pop-up window to deliver this warning and keep you legal.

9.8: GOING LIVE

After your site is fully set up and you've received inventory at your warehouse, you're ready to go live! You should place some test orders to ensure that your website, shopping cart, checkout, payment processors, apps, warehouse API integration, and automated emails are all functioning as intended. Once you get all the kinks worked out by placing test orders, you're ready to publish your website and see what happens!

CHAPTER 10:

MARKETING

Womp womp... your store went live and nobody showed up! Don't worry, this happens to everyone. You can't expect people to magically find your new store within the vast expanse of the internet. You have to actively drive traffic to your store through marketing and advertising.

Throughout this chapter we'll explore some marketing tactics to help you drive qualified shoppers to your store. The most important part of selling a product is first getting people to see it. Equally important is ensuring that the right people see it at the right time. Driving qualified traffic can be extremely expensive and difficult, but it doesn't have to be if you're clever with your marketing and you have a great product.

Great marketing can be done both digitally and offline. The most successful companies leverage both avenues for a well-rounded marketing presence. However, in the current digital economy it is often most effective for small brands to focus on digital campaigns due to the ability to find targeted audiences, make instant adjustments, and measure campaign results in real time. Since this book is intended to help you get your first million dollars in sales, the majority of this chapter is focused on digital marketing tactics. You can buy billboards, sponsor the X-Games®, and purchase full-page magazine ads later when your company is much larger.

10.1: DIGITAL MARKETING BASICS

The broad term "digital marketing" encompasses a number of more specific marketing disciplines including: public relations, digital advertising, search engine optimization, search engine marketing, influencer marketing, affiliate marketing, permission marketing, and organic social media marketing. Each of these disciplines will eventually become an important part of your business, but being really good at just one or two of them can often be enough to launch and grow a successful product brand.

The world of digital marketing is full of acronyms. These tend to make everything seem much more complicated and difficult than it actually is. I'm not saying marketing is easy – it's not. But, the principles and concepts are quite simple once you understand the jargon.

Let's walk through a few of the most common acronyms you'll run into in this chapter and throughout your digital marketing career.

AOV = Average Order Value. This is the average value of all orders placed on your website, or driven through a particular campaign over a specified period of time.

Conversion Rate = The average percentage of visitors who make a purchase on your website. If you had 1000 visitors this week and 20 of them made a purchase, your conversion rate is 2%.

CPA = Cost Per Acquisition. This is a measurement of the average cost of getting someone to perform a specific "action." With most product based companies the desired "action" is making a purchase. Under these circumstances, this is a measurement of the average cost of acquiring a new customer.

CPC = Cost Per Click. This is a measurement of your average cost to get 1 person to click on your ad.

CPM = Cost Per Thousand Impressions. This is a measurement of the cost to display your ad 1,000 times.

KPI = Key Performance Indicators. These are the metrics you care about most, plan to measure, and will use to determine whether or not your campaigns are successful.

PPC = Pay Per Click. This is an acronym used to describe an advertising model where you pay for every click your ad receives.

PR = Public relations. This typically deals with organic, earned media coverage rather than paid-for coverage.

ROAS = Return on Ad Spend. A ratio showing the amount of revenue generated per dollar spent on advertising. If you earn $550 by spending $100 on advertising, your ROAS is 5.5:1

ROI = Return on Investment. Similar to ROAS but can apply to the amount spent on anything, not just advertising spend

SEM = Search Engine Marketing. The process of getting more traffic or visibility to a website primarily through paid search engine advertising

SEO = Search Engine Optimization. The process of getting popular search engines, like Google, to list your website in the top organic results for various search terms.

There are dozens of other digital marketing terms and acronyms that you could take the time to learn, but this pretty much covers the basics that you'll really need to know and understand.

The overall goals of digital marketing for a product company are to grow consumer awareness, drive traffic to your product, and ultimately generate product sales. There are many ways to go about this and there's no definitively right or wrong way – any method that efficiently achieves these goals is the right way.

Every product, brand, and company will have to approach digital marketing a little differently. Some products are highly noteworthy, and these may be able to earn enough organic media coverage to launch and grow a brand without ever spending a dollar on marketing. Some entrepreneurs may really excel at social networking, or they may even have large social media followings already. These companies might build their empires using various social media platforms. Some products may have a very high conversion rate when shown to the right audience, and companies making these products can often scale up very quickly using digital ads on platforms like Facebook and Instagram. There is no universal recipe for marketing success. The right answer to your marketing challenge is the one that works, and it can often require some experimentation to figure out what that is.

In the pages that follow we'll walk through the various digital marketing disciplines and tactics commonly employed by successful product companies. It's important to understand that, regardless of where you find your strength, you should be employing all of these tactics throughout your business to some extent. Having all of these marketing channels running simultaneously will allow you to divert funds toward the channel that's working most efficiently for you. If you're going to spend on marketing, you should spend where it's most impactful. Additionally, focusing exclusively on a single marketing channel makes you vulnerable to changing consumer habits, changing platform rules or algorithms, or even changing commerce laws. The field of digital marketing evolves extremely quickly and strategies that worked a year ago will often not work today. With this in mind, you should always be testing new marketing channels and tactics to grow your business.

10.2: PUBLIC RELATIONS (PR)

In the product world, public relations is primarily concerned with growing product awareness through earned media. I'm sure you've seen the results of successful PR efforts – articles about a great new tech product or a roundup of the "Ten Best Backpacks for Back-To-School." It may seem like the companies who land their products in these articles just got lucky, but it actually requires effort and strategy to be amongst the chosen few. The sum of these efforts comprises the discipline of PR.

Many successful brands have been launched and built on earned media alone. Since earned media coverage is typically free, it can be an extremely powerful tool for growing a brand from nothing. However, this typically only works for very noteworthy or trendy products that editors and writers are excited to cover. If a writeup on your product wouldn't make for an interesting article to a specific audience, you shouldn't expect it to receive a lot of media coverage. On the contrary, if your product is noteworthy and would be a topic of interest for many audiences, you might want to consider hiring a PR agency as a primary marketing tactic.

I'm a big fan of DIY marketing, but PR is very difficult to DIY. Effective PR requires having a working relationship and an open communication line with industry writers and editors. It requires having insight into the articles they plan to write in the coming weeks and months. It also requires having fresh content to serve these writers constantly, so that there is value for them in maintaining a working relationship with you. If you're a single company that launches a few products a year, it can be extremely difficult to deliver the value necessary to get the ear of these busy writers and editors. You'll mostly just be an annoyance that somehow got their email address. However, if you're a PR agency who represents dozens of different companies and you always have the inside scoop on the latest gear that hasn't even launched yet, it's a whole different story. The power of the PR agency lies in the fact that they represent a lot of clients. They see all the new products long before they come out, and they can usually arrange to get writers a sample of their client's product before it even hits the market. These agencies have the scoop and the hookup, so it's no wonder writers and editors are willing to work closely with them! Having a good PR agency will cost you a sizable monthly fee (typically $2,000 - $6,000/month) but it can often pay that back in multiples if you receive a few good placements.

PR placements can come in a lot of flavors. You could land a 10 second mention on a popular morning TV show, or a spot in a product roundup in the Delta Airlines Sky Magazine. You might see your product placed on a popular gear blog like Uncrate, Gear Junkie, or Hi Consumption. It can even come in the form of industry awards, celebrity mentions, or a product review from a popular YouTube® reviewer. If your product strikes a chord with a certain audience, PR can be one of the most cost-effective means of growing your business.

When selecting a PR agency, you want to select one that specializes in your industry as much as possible. There are agencies that excel in every industry imaginable, from beauty products to industrial technology, and everything in between. You should seek out a specialist because they need to have the relationships and contacts within your industry to be effective. If you make the world's hardest-hitting baseball bat but hire an agency that typically specializes in food products, do you think they'll have the contact information of the gear editor at *Sports Illustrated*? Probably not! This is why you should choose someone who specializes in products like yours.

In my experience, the best way to gauge the future performance of an agency is by speaking to some of their existing clients. Any agency that is serious about earning your business should be able to provide a few references for you to contact. Have their references had a great experience? Do they plan to retain the agency again next year? How long have they been with this agency? These are all excellent questions to ask their references to gain some insight into the quality of service you can expect. If you don't get a "hell yes" about the agency in question, keep looking until you do. You shouldn't settle for middle-of-the-road performers when there are truly exceptional agencies out there who are eager to earn your business.

Once you have a proper agency working on your behalf, you should expect to ship out a lot of samples. Most writers will want to see and use the product before they tell their audience about it, and you can't expect them to pay for it. This can be challenging if your product is extremely expensive to produce because the cost of the sample may not be worth the value of the coverage. This can also apply to not-so-expensive products if you have the opportunity to send a sample to a very small media source. You should evaluate each opportunity as it arises, but to run an effective PR campaign you will need to be liberal with free samples.

Earned media can be an amazing tool for growing certain product brands, but it's also a bit unpredictable, inconsistent, and mostly out of your control. Paid media, on the other hand, is fully within your control and can sometimes produce predictable, stable, and scalable results for your business.

The most common form of paid media happens through the process of digital advertising.

10.3: DIGITAL ADVERTISING

What would you do if you could hand me a dollar and I would consistently hand you three in return? If you have any sense, you'd hand me every dollar you have as quickly as possible. Then you'd start handing me all the newly earned dollars to get that 3x return on those too. Pretty soon you'll find that you've invested an enormous amount of money in this scheme, but you've made significantly more than you invested. This is the idea behind paid advertising and it's exactly why the advertising budgets of many successful companies are so much larger than the budgets of other departments. If you can spend a dollar on ads and get several in return, it just makes sense to spend a lot on ads.

Digital advertising is essentially paying to place your ad in front of a potential customer with the goal of achieving a desired outcome; typically selling them your product. This is a very big topic that can, and does, fill the pages of many dedicated books, so you'll want to continue your research and learning well beyond the overview presented here. You can choose to advertise on an endless number of digital platforms and there are just as many types and tactics of digital advertising as there are platforms on which to place them. For the purposes of this book, we will cover the most common platforms and methods employed by the majority of successful product companies. This doesn't mean you shouldn't look at other options – you should always be experimenting with new ways to achieve your marketing goals. But, this book is only intended to help you get through your first million dollars in sales so we'll be sticking to the most common, proven platforms and methods available to date. Also, we're going to give search engine marketing (SEM) its own section in this chapter, so that will be excluded from this section even though it's an important aspect of digital advertising.

There are essentially two main categories of digital ads: Prospecting and retargeting. Prospecting ads are intended to gain new customers. The targets of prospecting ads have never seen your product before, so you're starting from zero. Prospecting campaigns typically have a lower ROAS (return on ad spend) than other ads because customers don't often buy something the first time they see it. They usually require some time to warm up to a new idea before spending their hard-earned dollars on it. Retargeting ads, on the other hand, are intended to make the sale to customers who are already aware of your product. These ads are most often served to recent website visitors who left without converting, or people on your email list who are yet to make a purchase. If you sell a non-durable product like moisturizing lotion or protein bars, a retargeting ad could involve pushing customers who haven't bought in the last 30 days to buy again. There are dozens of ad types within these two categories, but any ad you serve will likely fall into one of these two camps.

The collection of potential customers in varying stages of awareness and purchase intent make up your digital advertising "funnel." This is a commonly used word to describe the customer acquisition process starting with the widest audience who could conceivably buy your product and narrowing down to those who will buy your product. You need to be intentional with your ad content to generate an effective digital advertising funnel. The process starts with prospecting campaigns designed to spread awareness and attract qualified traffic to your website. You probably won't make the sale on the customer's first visit, so your goal here is to build product awareness and get the attention of people who may eventually be interested in what you're offering. This type of prospecting campaign is often called an "awareness campaign" because the main goal is to make potential new customers aware of your product. This is also referred to as "filling the top of the funnel" because you're adding new prospects to push through your advertising funnel toward conversion, similar to pouring water into the top of a funnel. A good prospecting campaign will result in a large volume of interested visitors to your website. From there, customers enter the "consideration" phase where they begin to make decisions around whether they're interested in your offering at all, or they begin research to compare your offering to that of your competitors. At this point, you start serving these prospects retargeting ads designed to demonstrate product value and bring them closer to purchase. You want to guide them through the consideration process with the timely delivery of ads that push them past potential sticking points. This stage is commonly called "mid-funnel" because these customers are already aware of your product but might not be ready to purchase yet. As their interest grows and they visit your site a time or two more, they become lower-funnel prospects. Ads to these prospects are often called "conversion campaigns" because they're designed to generate a purchase. Ads should be served frequently to prospects in this stage of the process and should include strong call-to-action messaging like "buy now." Some companies even use discounts to get these customers over the finish line. This entire process represents your digital advertising funnel. Properly managing your funnel and the prospects within is critical to your future digital marketing success. Fortunately, there are several platforms and services available to help you dial in your audience and serve them the right message at the right time.

Let's start with the Facebook and Instagram advertising platform. As you may or may not know, Facebook acquired Instagram in 2012 and ads for both platforms are managed through Facebook Business Manager. These services have billions of regular users and retain an enormous amount of data on each of those users. This is what makes these platforms so powerful for advertisers like yourself. If you're trying to target females in New York City between the age of 25 and 34 with an interest in photography, you can do exactly that through Facebook. These services are constantly monitoring what every user engages with, reads, clicks on, and likes, so they know a lot about their users. They also have their users' attention. The billions of users on these platforms spend billions of hours staring at Facebook and Instagram content every day. This rare and powerful combination of attention and data makes Facebook one of the most powerful advertising platforms on the planet. For a price, they will allow you to use their database and buy their users' attention. You can specify your target audience and the exact content you would like to serve and, through Facebook Business Manager, you can start driving sales that same day.

To get started you must first create a Facebook Business Manager account. Then you need to connect your new ad account to your Shopify website using the Facebook "pixel." The Facebook pixel is a piece of code you install on your website that tracks and transmits customer behavior back to the Business Manager ad platform. This connection provides critical data that shows how effective your campaigns are and enables you and the platform to dial in your ads and audiences to achieve your goals. There is a dedicated field in the Shopify backend where you simply paste the pixel code that Facebook provides you. Once your account is setup and your site is connected, you're ready to start building ads.

The most important part of running a successful campaign on the Facebook platform is selecting the right audience. One way to ensure you won't be successful is by assuming everyone in the world is interested in your product and serving ads to an extremely wide audience. Instead, you need to focus your advertising dollars on those who are the most likely to buy your product and slowly expand your audience from there. There are a couple of good ways to define an audience in the Facebook platform. The first method is by simply dialing in the demographics and interests of your potential customer using the options available in the Business Manager platform. Do you remember your muse from Chapter 3? If you already defined their demographics and interests, that's probably a great place to start. It's a rare and exceptional product that can get a good ROAS at a decent scale using this type of audience, but it definitely does happen. When it does, you're really on to something good!

Another great method for building an audience is by using "look-alikes." Look-alike audiences are built by selecting or uploading a specific set of individuals and letting the Facebook platform serve your ads to other people that share similar characteristics, interests, and habits. Facebook has an extraordinary amount of data on each individual user – much more than you could ever take advantage of by simply dialing in demographics and interests. When you use a look-alike audience, the system is using more of these datapoints to find prospects who most closely match those that you selected or uploaded. You have the ability to select how closely the prospective audience must match your dataset. If you select a narrow 2% match, meaning that only the closest matching 2% of platform users will be served, your audience will be relatively small but the ROAS should be higher than if you select a 10% match. Increasing the match percentage will open your ads up to a larger audience but this will often reduce effectiveness since your ads are less targeted. Successful digital advertising is about finding that balance between ROAS and scale.

It's typically most effective to build a look-alike audience using people who have already performed the desired action. For example, if you have a brand that makes gardening supplies and you're building a campaign to sell your new self-watering flower pot, the best possible look-alike audience will most likely be built from the dataset of customers who have already purchased this exact flower pot. The system will digest the data and find similarities between those who have purchased this product. Then it will serve ads to potential new customers who also share these similarities. You need at least 100 people to have a statistically significant dataset, and it's recommended that you start with 1,000 to make it really effective. This can present a problem for new companies or new products with little purchase history. When you find yourself in this situation you can move further up the funnel. Continuing with the garden supply company example, you might be able to use the data from purchases of the old version of the flowerpot, or a different model that has more purchase history. If this isn't an option you can start with the data of everyone who has purchased on your website in the last 60 days. Still not enough data? Use the dataset containing everyone who visited your website in the last 30 or 90 days. These are all valid and effective ways to build a look-alike audience that will probably still outperform an audience you build using demographics and interests.

When you're just starting out, it can be very difficult to drive enough traffic and purchase activity to acquire the dataset necessary to run a good look-alike campaign. You may find that you have to advertise using only demographics and interests until you get enough purchase data to start building look-alike audiences. When doing this, you can expect your ROAS to be pretty low while you're trying to build up your data. You may even be working at a loss until you can get enough data to build a better audience, and that's ok. Like all things in a product business, advertising is challenging, competitive, and expensive. It will require some trial and error to get right and you should expect to spend some money building your funnel in the beginning.

The process of keeping your look-alike audience targeted but expanding the scale is a balancing act. I recommend you manage it by setting some specific minimum ROAS goals that, when met, yield an acceptable level of profit for your company. You'll then start each campaign with the narrowest audience possible and expand the audience until ROAS drops to that minimum goal. This method allows you to test, dial, and scale new campaigns to their full potential without any significant risk. In the best case scenario, your ROAS never drops below the minimum threshold as you broaden the audience and you realize that you have a highly scalable campaign. In the worst case scenario, you start the campaign with a modest budget to the most targeted audience and it never exceeds the minimum threshold so you kill it and try something different. You end up with only modest losses and some new learnings to incorporate into your next campaign.

There are other powerful ways to drive conversions outside the Facebook platform. You've probably seen the ads that follow you around on every website you go to after you've looked at certain products. Those are called display retargeting ads and they help to keep your product on the top of a potential customer's mind for a certain period of time. Customers have a short memory – they often look at a product and then forget about it entirely, even if they're initially interested. If you can keep your product on the top of their mind, you drastically increase your chances of turning a shopper into a buyer.

Display retargeting ads are typically bought and served through Google or other third-party retargeting companies like AdRoll or Criteo. There are a number of these providers out there and they all provide a similar service; an interface to build or upload ads and serve them to prior website visitors who meet the criteria of your choosing. You can choose to retarget everyone who visits your site, or just those who viewed certain products. You can retarget only those who spent a certain amount of time on your site, or who viewed 3 or more items during their visit, for example. You should expect your ROAS to improve as you narrow your audience to target the more engaged shoppers.

These services work on a bidding system, so the price to serve your ad changes throughout the year. To get your ads to show up, you need to bid more than anyone else for a specific customer. The retargeting platforms make this reasonably easy to manage and provide estimates on what you'll need to bid to win placement. Many also offer an intelligent auto-bid system to make management even easier, although the effectiveness varies.

Gauging the true ROAS of a digital advertising campaign isn't always as simple as it seems. There are several tricks that ad platforms and service providers sometimes use to make you think they're providing more value than they are. There are also some customer habits that make accurate measurement difficult.

One common trick to be aware of is gauging ROAS by using a "Veiw-Through Conversion" metric (VTC). When tracking view-through conversions, the ad campaign will take credit for anyone who converted within a certain timeframe after having an ad show up on a webpage they view. We all know that most ads, especially display ads on the side or top of random websites, go unnoticed most of the time. Also, many ads are placed further down the page (referred to as "below the fold") and the campaign may take credit for a conversion when the customer didn't even scroll down far enough to see the ad. Additionally, many platforms start off with a 30 day conversion window, meaning they take credit for any conversion up to 30 days after showing someone an ad. Giving a campaign full credit for a conversion under these circumstances is extremely generous towards the campaign, and probably doesn't accurately reflect the ROAS your campaign is achieving. It does, however, make the ad company look really good so you'll continue spending a lot of money with them. Beware of this common trick and don't evaluate your ROAS using view-through conversion metrics with long conversion windows. If you choose to use view-through metrics at all, change the conversion window to 1 day to increase the odds that the ad actually had some influence over the purchase.

A better option may be to use a "Click-Through Conversion" metric (CTC). Using this metric, the campaign only gets credit when someone clicks the ad and subsequently purchases within a given timeframe. While you probably won't over-credit your campaigns using this evaluation metric, you might risk under-crediting them. This is where consumer habits can make it difficult to accurately gauge advertising success metrics. Some customers will see an ad and remember that they do want to purchase the item. Instead of clicking the ad and buying the product, they do a quick web search for your company and convert without interacting with the ad at all. The ad was successful but the campaign did not get credit for the conversion. This behavior is relatively common, so the actual ROAS of a display retargeting campaign usually lies somewhere between the reported click-through ROAS and the view-through ROAS. Figuring out exactly where is virtually impossible.

Another common challenge occurs when your products are sold at other online retailers or third-party platforms like Amazon. The customers you target may prefer to buy from Amazon, for example, after you win them with your ad. While this still adds to your bottom line, the campaign doesn't get credit for the conversion if it happens on another website. This means your ROAS data will show a lower return than you're actually achieving.

There is currently no great way to accurately account for the intricacies of customer behavior, and it's only going to get more difficult as policy and legislation around online privacy increases. For these reasons, running a successful digital ad campaign still requires a lot of instinct and good judgement that only comes with practice. You may consider starting by using relatively conservative conversion metrics like a 7-day click-through only. This will ensure you're getting the value you think you are from your campaign. You can consider loosening the metrics as you gain experience and understanding of ad platforms and behaviors of your specific customer.

Google Analytics (commonly referred to as "G.A.") is another great tool that can help you unravel some of the mystery surrounding your ad campaigns. This service offers a number of valuable tools to help you understand the flow of traffic to and through your website. It can account for data from a number of different advertising platforms and services to give you a better picture of what's actually working and what isn't. I encourage you to set up and use Google Analytics to help evaluate all of your digital marketing campaigns and generally improve the effectiveness of your website.

10.4: SEARCH ENGINE MARKETING (SEM)

Search engine marketing is another extremely powerful tool for both prospecting and retargeting ad campaigns. The most popular search engine marketing tool is Google Ads (formerly called Google AdWords). You can find similar tools for other search engines like Bing and Yahoo, but the volumes are much lower since fewer people use these search engines.

Like most modern digital ads, search engine ads are bought and served using a bidding system. Each advertiser places a bid on a specific keyword and the cost is tallied on a pay per click basis (PPC). The bid is the maximum amount an advertiser is willing pay to have their ad served when someone searches for a particular word or phrase. However, the highest bidder doesn't necessarily win. In order to ensure the search results (ads included) are relevant to the user's search, Google weights each ad by relevance. If your ad is not highly relevant to a keyword you're bidding on, you may have to pay several times more than someone who is serving more relevant content. This system ultimately works out better for everyone. Users get more relevant search results and advertisers are rewarded for serving relevant content. Let's face it; you wouldn't get a good ROAS by serving ads for blue jeans when someone searched for a spatula anyways.

There are many types of search engine ads but the most relevant for our needs are the traditional PPC text ad and the shopping ad. I'm sure you're familiar with both. The traditional text ad shows up above or beside the organic search results. If you search "flights to Hawaii" you will undoubtedly get ads for various booking sites, travel agencies, and airlines served ahead of the actual search results. Shopping ads are a bit different. These are the thumbnail photos with listed prices that show up at the top of a SERP (Search Engine Results Page) showing you various product offerings that are similar to what you searched for. If you search for "scented candles" you will almost certainly see a row of scented candle offerings at the top of the page, and these are shopping ads. Both of these ad types can be set up through the Google Ad Manager.

Search engine advertising can yield a comparably high ROAS as a prospecting tool – often higher than most other prospecting means. This is because the traffic you are bidding on has already been filtered. The potential customer had to search for a keyword that is relevant to your product for your ad to be served, so they're probably interested or in the market to buy a product like yours already. Now you just need to convince them that your offering is the one to choose. Compare this to prospecting through social media advertising where you're serving ads to anyone who may only have a general interest in your product and probably isn't actively looking to make a purchase at the time. As you can imagine, it's much easier to convert the customer who was already planning to make a similar purchase.

The key to success with search engine text ads is ensuring your product is highly relevant to the keywords you choose to bid against, and writing compelling copy that instantly resonates with the person who initiated the search. This will require some research and some trial and error. You can do your homework on various keywords using the Google Keyword Planner. You can also explore dynamic text ads that help fill in gaps in your keywords and provide more precise and relevant copy to search engine users.

Search engine shopping ads share a similar benefit of having pre-filtered traffic, and they provide an even faster way to put your product in front of the customer. They will typically show a photo and the price of your item directly in the ad. They can, however, be quite competitive. Your product is placed in a lineup alongside your competitors with little means to differentiate your offering. In addition to relevant keywords, you'll need compelling photography, good product design, and an appealing pricepoint to succeed with shopping ads.

The topic of search engine advertising is so large and complex that it would require its own book for anything more than a brief overview. I recommend doing extensive research and reading on PPC search engine advertising before you start because you can waste money very quickly if you don't know what you're doing. Fortunately, there are many books dedicated to the topic and there's a lot of great information available online as well.

If all this starts to feel like too much, you can always hire an agency to manage your digital advertising program. There are literally thousands of these agencies out there and they can be found through a quick google search. If you decide to hire an agency, you should still take the time to learn as much as possible about digital advertising so you can manage them properly and set reasonable success metrics for the agency. Both you and your agency need to agree on what success or failure looks like before you start working together. You also need to speak the language and understand the general concepts of digital advertising to effectively manage and work with your account manager.

As always when hiring an agency, contact their references and make sure they have only great things to say before you sign the contract. Also, be sure you interview your future account manager thoroughly before you sign on – they're the one who will be doing the work on your account. Don't fall in love with the agency's salesperson because you'll probably never hear from them again after you sign up.

Once you've brought an agency on board, never take their numbers at face value. They often use reporting metrics that are most favorable to them rather than using what is most accurate. It's imperative that you define the ROAS metrics and reporting windows so you don't get fleeced. Don't be afraid to call them out when they're using a 60-day view-through conversion window. You know that's bogus and they do too, but they'll often try to get away with it if you let them. Most of their customers don't know what that means, so it works more often than not. Be diligent, ask questions, and clearly communicate your needs and expectations. This is the only way to succeed with a digital advertising agency.

10.5: SEARCH ENGINE OPTIMIZATION

Another important aspect of driving traffic to your website is search engine optimization or SEO. SEO is the process of improving the quantity or quality of organic traffic that reaches your site through search engine queries. Most shoppers never make it past the first page of search results, so getting your product listed on page 1 is critical. Good SEO is vital to the long-term success of your business because the traffic is free and, often, highly qualified.

There was a time when clever marketers could trick the search engine algorithms and quickly move certain sites to the first page of search results for specific keywords. These tactics are referred to as "black hat" SEO tactics, and those days are long gone. Most of those black hat tactics are now penalized by major search engines, meaning that using them will actually lower your chances of ever reaching the front page. Today, there are few shortcuts. The road to the first page of search results requires work, time, and diligently following some general best-practices.

The work starts with research and planning of the keywords and keyword phrases that are relevant to your website. Google Keyword Planner is a great tool for the keyword research process. Then you need to ensure those keywords make it into your website content, especially the product pages. You also need to regularly develop high-quality, keyword-rich content for your site. If done right, this content will attract search engine traffic over time. Better content will yield better results. Have you ever wondered why product companies go through the extra effort to write a bunch of informational articles for their blog? This is why! These articles aren't focused on immediately selling a product. The goal is to attract search engine traffic using high quality content so your overall site ranking improves.

PR is another key element to improve your SEO. PR generates high-quality backlinks, which are one of the most important metrics search engines use to rank websites. Backlinks are external websites linking to your website. One of the most prominent black hat SEO techniques of yesteryear involved adding hundreds of backlinks to a bunch of spammy websites that only existed to contain backlinks. The search engines caught on and this is now penalized. Nowadays the quality of the websites that link back to your site is extremely important. Good PR should result in news coverage and product reviews on high quality websites that all link back to your site. This generates the high-quality backlinks you need to improve your website ranking.

Great content alone isn't usually enough to reach the first page of search results. Remember, there are millions of people competing for this coveted position. To win a spot on the first page, you also need to follow some best practices.

First and foremost, your website needs to be discoverable by search engine "crawlers." Crawlers are bots deployed by search engine providers that bounce around the internet from link to link building an index of categorized and ranked URLs. When your site is brand new, there probably aren't any other websites linking in. Without this path to your site, it's unlikely your site will be discovered. To remedy this, create some links to your site wherever you can. Use PR to get some coverage and, hopefully, links to your site. Last, you should manually request a crawl from Google or submit a sitemap if your website is large. You can find detailed instructions on how to request a crawl or submit a sitemap here: https://developers.google.com/search/docs/advanced/crawling/ask-google-to-recrawl

The user experience on your website is another critical aspect of SEO. If the content someone seeks isn't immediately and obviously available, they will most likely leave pretty quickly (commonly called "bouncing"). To prevent bouncing you should ensure your website is easy to navigate and the content the user seeks is immediately available when they click through. You should also pay close attention to your website loading speeds. Research indicates that load speeds of 5 seconds have a bounce rate over four times higher than sites that load in 2 seconds or less. If a search engine notices that users are frequently bouncing from your site, it will assume your site does not contain content that's useful and relevant to their search. This results in a poor ranking and prevents you from moving closer to the first page. Google provides some useful tools for analyzing and improving your website load speeds here: https://developers.google.com/speed/pagespeed/insights/. You also need to build your site on a "responsive" template so it seamlessly adjusts to mobile traffic. Over half of global web traffic now occurs on mobile devices so the search engines penalize sites that do not optimize the experience for mobile users.

In addition to showing up early in search results, you also need to ensure people actually click the links to your site. The best way to do this is with a good meta description. A meta description is the small paragraph under each search engine result that describes the webpage you will go to if you click that link. If you chose to build your store using Shopify, this can be easily edited for each page under the "Edit Website SEO" field at the bottom of the page or product creation template. Your meta description should be a brief, accurate, and compelling description of the product or page that it links to. This may be your only opportunity to snag a potential visitor, so having a good description is key to taking advantage of your SEO success.

As you would probably expect, there are hundreds of agencies that will gladly assist you with SEO for your website. Be very careful in vetting these agencies because some may still use black hat tactics for quick results at the expense of your long-term success. A professional SEO agency will be able to dig deeper and do more than what is covered in this overview. They can help maximize short-term and long-term results. However, this may not be necessary for your business. Given the current state of SEO and how effectively Google and other search engines find and rank quality content without perfect SEO practices, I don't feel that hiring an SEO agency is the best use of a lean startup's capital. You may want to hire an agency short-term to get things set up and running properly, but continued SEO support is probably not necessary if you're willing to put in some work yourself. If you choose to go the DIY route, there are some fantastic online resources to improve your knowledge and hone your SEO skills. A quick google search about any SEO topic will produce a litany of useful results and resources.

10.6: INFLUENCER MARKETING

Influencer marketing is a type of social media marketing that leverages the reach and influence of famous individuals or experts in a given field. Typically, an influencer will endorse or even claim to use a product in exchange for compensation. This can be an extremely powerful prospecting tool if the influencer's opinion is revered and trusted by their audience. As of this writing, Instagram and YouTube are the most commonly used platforms for influencer marketing campaigns.

Influencer marketing was all the rage from 2014 to 2019. Many popular brands were built overnight on influencer marketing alone. The return on investment was often excellent and "being an influencer" blossomed into a legitimate career path for tens-of-thousands of people. The excitement and potential has since declined, but this can still be a very powerful marketing strategy for many brands.

Influencer marketing typically requires a direct relationship between the brand and the influencer. These connections are often made through direct messages on Instagram or other social media platforms. From there, an agreement will be made to exchange product promotion for some level of compensation. You'll then send your product to the influencer so they can get some content of them using your product and then they'll fulfil their end of the deal – posting and promoting your content to their audience.

The early days of influencer marketing were dominated by small brands who could attain a significant revenue impact through their direct relationships with influencers. Building these relationships and setting up these campaigns one influencer at a time requires a lot of time and energy. This lack of scalability deterred the big brands for several years, until they realized they could skip the relationship building if they just paid more than anyone else. This drove up the market value of the influencers and, more impactfully, eroded the trust of their audiences. All the influencers suddenly switched from promoting authentic small brands to the largest beer and car brands in the world. Their audience saw through it and trust was lost. Not only was influencer marketing then more expensive than ever, it was also less effective.

A common mistake is to assume that the most famous influencer is the best one to promote your brand. This thinking is a near-certain way to bleed money. Considering the history of influencer marketing, the best influencer to partner with is actually the one that has the most relevant audience and the most trust among that audience. For this reason, many brands are now turning to "micro-influencers" for a more authentic campaign that often yields a better return on investment. Micro-influencers often have very concentrated and engaged audiences of 1,000 to 50,000 individuals. They also tend to have much higher distribution rates than larger influencers. This means that the platform might serve their content to 40% or more of their total followers or subscribers, instead of the 5-10% often seen with larger accounts. Micro-influencer marketing can often give a brand much more bang for the buck and result in a much higher conversion percentage than traditional influencer marketing.

One of the most impactful forms of influencer marketing comes in the form of product review videos on YouTube. There are professional product reviewers for most product categories, and getting a positive video review from them can be very powerful. This type of influencer marketing isn't just a short-term prospecting tool like most other forms of influencer marketing. Video reviews can actually increase your conversion rate for the lifetime of the product. This happens because many customers may be interested in your product, but they just want to know a little more about it before they make the purchase. These detailed video reviews are sought out by interested customers and a positive review from a trusted source can push them over the finish line. Because video reviews provide lasting value for a product or brand, these influencers will often agree to an "affiliate commission" payment structure instead of payment upfront. This affiliate marketing arrangement can be beneficial for both the brand and the influencer.

10.7: AFFILIATE MARKETING

Affiliate marketing is where brands share a percentage of the income that results from the traffic driven by writers, editors, reviewers, or influencers. This commission is typically tracked and paid through an affiliate network like AvantLink, Skimlinks, Amazon Associates, or ShareASale, to name a few. Typical affiliate commissions range from 5-30% of the sale depending on the industry, but most industries land in the 10-15% range.

By using custom affiliate links to your website, affiliate networks make it possible to track when a buying customer reaches your site through an affiliate partner. Affiliate networks automate the monthly commission payments to your affiliate partners and bill you a single amount for all the combined payments and their service fee. Affiliate platform service fees are typically billed as a percentage of what is paid out to your affiliate partners, but with a monthly minimum in place. You can expect to spend a few hundred dollars per month to maintain access to a quality affiliate network.

One of the best aspects of affiliate marketing is that commission is only paid when results are achieved. This ensures you don't end up paying for ineffective work. Affiliate marketing is also cash flow positive since you get paid by your customer before you have to pay your affiliate partners. At the same time, affiliates only want to cover your product if they think it will sell well because they won't get paid unless it does. This can be a great arrangement for all parties involved if, and only if, you have a great selling product.

Affiliate marketing is a great way to get media coverage that appears to be organic. This organic-looking coverage is often much more powerful than a traditional advertisement because the reader thinks it's coming from a trusted, unbiased third party. Most consumers aren't aware of affiliate marketing and they don't realize that the media is often getting paid to generate content reviewing or recommending certain products. This disconnect results in more authentic-seeming content and, often, good results.

Like anything else, you can't just sign up for an affiliate network and expect quality affiliate partners to come knocking on your door. These programs take effort to build and run effectively. You will need to seek out relevant publishers and content creators to invite to your affiliate program. This can be done through the backend of your affiliate network or even by reaching out to them directly. You need to provide them with content that they can modify and publish with minimal effort. You also need to offer an appealing commission percentage so it's worth their time to write about your product over someone else's. Remember, their time is as limited as yours and there are tens-of-thousands of products they could potentially cover for an affiliate commission. You have to make yours easier to cover and more financially appealing than most others if you expect to get in on the action.

An affiliate relationship can be a great way to work with product review sites or channels. As mentioned previously, these reviews can provide value to your customers for the entire lifespan of a product, so an affiliate partner can make a lot of money over time on just a single product review. This makes for an appealing arrangement for the brand and the product reviewer.

You can also use affiliate commission as part of your influencer marketing program. Most influencers will require cash payment upfront, but you might be able to negotiate a lower rate if you add an affiliate commission component to their compensation structure. Additionally, if part of their payment relies on the performance of their promotion, they'll probably give their best effort in promoting your product to maximize their income. This can help protect against lackluster delivery, which is not an uncommon issue in the influencer marketing world.

Affiliate marketing really shines as an augmentation to your PR strategy. If you already have a great PR agency working to get media coverage on your behalf, adding a small affiliate commission can be a great way to boost the amount of coverage you secure. For example, let's say that you design and sell women's swim suits and a popular digital publication is planning an article about the "Top 10 Beach Looks of 2021." The writer has literally thousands of potential swim suits to choose from for their article, but if your PR team has already done the work to ensure yours is in consideration and it comes with a small affiliate commission that others don't have, your product is very likely to get featured.

It's very unlikely that you will build your business on an affiliate program alone. These programs are typically used as powerful and effective add-ons to your other marketing tactics because they're not as scalable as many other marketing strategies. On the upside, you only pay for results and the process is typically cash flow positive. All things considered, affiliate marketing is an excellent addition or augmentation to your greater marketing plan.

10.8: PERMISSION MARKETING THROUGH EMAIL AND TEXT MESSAGES

Email and text message (SMS) marketing campaigns can be an extremely effective way to nurture customer relationships and drive revenue. Many companies find that these channels yield the best return on investment of any of their marketing strategies. Email and SMS campaigns are commonly referred to as "permission marketing" because the recipient must opt in before you can start delivering your message. Permission marketing gives you the opportunity to engage your customer directly, show them what your brand is all about, inform customers of sales and promotions, and generally remind them that you exist from time to time. The fact that every individual on your list had enough interest to opt in to receiving your marketing messages means that you have a highly curated audience that is very likely to convert in the future. All of these things combine to make email and SMS campaigns extremely valuable and effective.

Email marketing campaigns are usually managed through email marketing platforms like Klayvio, Mailchimp, or Constant Contact. There are a lot of these platforms to choose from and they all offer similar services with slightly different capabilities or specialties. Most major email marketing platforms have a Shopify plugin so they can integrate seamlessly with your Shopify store. This can be very useful for important automations that will significantly increase your conversion rate. I recommend checking the Shopify App Store to ensure there is a pre-built integration for the email marketing platform you're considering before you make a commitment.

Many email marketing platforms are free to use until you reach a certain number of subscribers, making them very friendly for new businesses who are just getting started. These platforms give you a way to design compelling emails and send them to a large volume of subscribers at one time. They also provide some other useful features like the ability to segment and manage your subscribers, a legal means for your subscribers to unsubscribe, automated marketing flows, and scheduled email sends. All of these features are necessary to run an effective email marketing campaign.

When done well, email marketing should be about more than product pitches and company news. The truth is, nobody cares when your company wins an award. You should strive to deliver value to your subscribers' inbox, not self-centered spam that they won't care to read. Value can come in a lot of forms including industry news, entertaining stories, new product information, sales or promotions, or really any content your audience will be interested in consuming. By providing value, you get the opportunity to consistently engage your audience instead of being sent to the spam folder after the second email.

Getting sent to spam is a very bad thing. Each email account has something called an "IP reputation" which is basically a rating of how spammy your email account is. When someone tags your email as "junk" or "spam," this action is recorded by their email host and it has a negative impact to your IP reputation. If your IP reputation falls below a certain threshold, your emails will start to land in your subscribers' junk or spam folders instead of their inbox. Once your emails are being sent directly to the spam folder, your email marketing program is virtually worthless.

When you're first starting out it can be tempting to take shortcuts to grow your email list quickly. Some entrepreneurs will buy email lists from sketchy sources, or swap lists with other small businesses. These are bad practices that will seriously damage your IP reputation, and may even be illegal. A good rule for protecting your IP reputation is to never add someone to your permission marketing list unless they knowingly opted in. This will go a long way toward ensuring your emails don't get relegated to the spam folder.

Email automations are another great email marketing tool that you should use in your product business. Most email platforms offer automations and they're relatively simple to set up. One of the most common automations is the abandon cart email. This is often triggered and sent if someone starts the checkout process but does not hit the "submit order" button to finalize the order. A gentle reminder can often be enough to get the customer to complete their order. Some brands choose to provide a small discount to increase their odds of finalizing the sale. Other common automations include the Welcome Series, New Customer Series, and the Re-engagement Series. The first two are automated email flows designed specifically to welcome new subscribers or new customers to your brand family. These introductory emails should let new subscribers know what type of content they should expect to receive and give them some immediate value to make them want to stay subscribed. The goal of the welcome series is to warm up new subscribers immediately after they agree to receive emails from you. This reduces unsubscribes and improves your odds of effectively marketing to them in the future. The Re-Engagement Series can be set up to automatically send to customers or shoppers who have seemingly lost interest in your brand. Perhaps this is someone who hasn't opened one of your emails in 90 days or stopped buying from you 6 months ago. This automated series should be a last-ditch effort to get them to reengage before you remove them from your list. It is both expensive and harmful to your IP reputation to keep dead leads on your email list, so you should consider removing leads if your Re-Engagement Series fails to bring them back.

Text message marketing, also called SMS marketing, is pretty similar to email marketing in that both require the recipient to opt in, both are an opportunity to engage directly with the customer, and both have to potential to drive significant revenue. However, the content and management of the two platforms must be handled differently. Text messages are more invasive than emails because most people keep notifications active on their text messages and they're much more likely to check them immediately upon arrival. This makes SMS a very effective form of marketing, but subscribers will unsubscribe quickly if you don't provide adequate value. At the moment, it seems that SMS marketing is best used for notifying subscribers about promotions or sales, providing early access to new product launches, delivering coupons, or sending order tracking and delivery notifications. These are things that subscribers are typically excited to receive so you can generate revenue without having your whole list unsubscribe.

The most challenging part of email or SMS marketing is building your subscriber base. This has become significantly more difficult in recent years. Customers have become more protective of their inbox as the number of companies trying to email them has exploded. There are still a few effective ways to build your subscriber base, such as lead-generation ad campaigns, subscribe at checkout, subscription incentive pop-ups, and giveaways. A lead-generation ad campaign is a type of prospecting campaign with the goal of getting someone to subscribe to your email or SMS marketing list. This could be a very compelling piece of content that is incomplete, requiring them to subscribe to read the rest. It could be an offer for a free product or a discount on your product that will be emailed to them if they subscribe. Your goal is to cheaply collect subscribers and try to convert them later through your email campaigns. Subscribe at checkout is a very common method to grow your subscriber base with qualified leads. This tactic uses a pre-checked "subscribe" box during checkout so that anyone who purchases from you automatically subscribes to your email list unless they un-check the box. While not the most transparent method, it does add many qualified leads to your list. You can also have the box default to un-checked for a more honest and transparent experience. Subscription incentive pop-ups are the ubiquitous pop-up windows that offer you a small discount if you sign up to receive the brand's email or SMS marketing. These windows are annoying, but there's a good reason that they're used on nearly every ecommerce website – they work. This feature can often be set up through your email marketing platform. Giveaways are another common way to build your subscriber base. This typically involves partnering with a few like-minded companies to give away a valuable prize bundle to one lucky subscriber. Each company involved promotes the giveaway to their social media followers and email subscriber base. Participants must opt in to receiving emails from all companies involved in the giveaway to enter. At the end of the campaign, one person is chosen as the winner and they receive the prize bundle. This can often result in a large number of new leads, but it's not the best way to build an engaged subscriber base. Leads generated through giveaways are usually very low quality and those that aren't engaged should be removed from your list quicky to avoid damage to your IP reputation.

Another way to build your subscriber base is by marketing the value of your email content through your organic social media channels. If you can get your social media followers to subscribe to your email list, you're one step closer to turning a prospect into a customer.

10.9: ORGANIC SOCIAL MEDIA

Organic social media for your business involves the use of popular social media platforms like Facebook, Instagram, and Twitter to build awareness, improve engagement, and drive sales. Organic use of these platforms does not include your paid ads and promotions, so it's essentially free. Facebook and Instagram (especially Instagram) have become the dominant platforms for product companies in recent years, so we'll focus primarily on these two platforms. Social media can be an extremely powerful tool for a product brand. Many product empires have been built entirely on social media, but it's much more difficult now than it was in the past. If you're starting your product business now, you will probably need a multi-faceted marketing plan where organic social media comprises just one important piece of the puzzle.

Social media for your brand should be exactly that – social media. This is your opportunity to socialize with your customers and improve engagement. Customers will often get excited when a brand simply responds to their comment, sends them a message, or reposts their content. The social aspect of social media is one of the most important and most overlooked aspects of properly running a commercial social media account. You should also make efforts to post content that your audience will want to see and share. Avoid the temptation to post about your product all the time. Your social media account won't succeed if it's a constant stream of ads – nobody wants to sign up for that. Instead, use this as an opportunity to go beyond the product and show that you share values with your customer. You will generate sales over time by creating more engaged customers that act as ambassadors for your brand.

Social media platforms typically work by distributing your content to a percentage of people that "follow" your account. You won't see a big response to your posts if you don't have any followers, so you need to start by building an audience. There are a number of strategies and methods to increase your follower count, but you need to put in a little legwork before you deploy those tactics in order to be successful.

The first step to building your social media following is to populate your account with some high-quality content. When someone follows your account, they're essentially agreeing to receive the content that you'll serve in the future. Since your past posts are the best indication of your future posts, you need to have some content in place to show potential followers what they can expect to receive once they follow you. Nobody wants to follow an empty account.

Before you start populating your account with random content, you should make a plan. The content you post needs to reflect the values of your brand, appeal to your core audience, and provide some value to your followers. Value can come in a lot of forms including jokes and entertainment, useful information, inspiring photos, motivational advice, etc. Many successful accounts latch on to one particular type of content and use that consistency to build a curated audience. This can be extremely effective because the consistency ensures people know exactly what they're signing up for when they follow you. Other successful accounts will develop a personality for their brand and post things that this personality would post if it were an individual. This personality should align well with the muse you developed in Chapter 3. In addition to keeping you aligned with your core customer, this method helps to ensure you treat your business social media account like a true social media account instead of a platform for ads. There are many other strategies you can use to develop and curate content, but the important part is that you have a strategy so you avoid posting a hodge-podge of unrelated content that doesn't consistently appeal to your target audience.

Once you've back-populated some content, you're ready to start building your audience. The most organic way to build an audience is through incredible content that gets liked and shared by your followers. This method has become more difficult over time with the sheer volume of great content available. You have to create truly exceptional content to grow your account using this method nowadays. Another organic means to grow your account is through cross-promotion from your other social accounts, email list, and website. You should connect your social media account to your website and encourage people to visit and follow you. You can encourage your email subscribers to also follow you on social media. Or, you can ask followers on one social platform to follow you on another if you've managed to build an audience on a different social platform. These organic methods of growing an audience can be effective, but they can also be painfully slow when you're trying to grow a new business. This is especially true in current times when the reach of organic posts is much smaller than it once was. Now the platforms want you to pay to get your message out.

If you're looking to grow your audience more quickly, you should consider putting some money behind it. "Boosted content" is one option for reaching new audience members and potentially growing your following on Facebook and Instagram. You'll see the offer to "boost your post" right in your main feed. This can be a very easy way to gain some instant visibility and possibly some followers, but it's probably not the best method. If you plan to boost your content, make sure it's good content that will attract the right audience and leave them wanting more so they follow your account. Alternatively, you should consider running ads through the Business Manager to distribute your content and attract followers instead of boosting posts. While it's not quite as easy, this method will give you much more control over your audience and allow you to evaluate the success of your campaign through the Business Manager's metrics. As you know from section 10.3 on Digital Advertising, curating the audience and tracking the metrics are two of the most important aspects of running a successful campaign. An ad campaign designed to build a following will be different from an ad campaign designed to drive sales. Your goal is different so your strategy should also be different. You should choose to serve your most compelling content instead of a traditional product advertisement. Your call-to-action will be to follow your account instead of the usual "learn more," "shop now," or "buy now" messaging. With good content and a solid campaign strategy, you should be able to attract quality followers for a reasonable cost.

Another way to quickly build a social following is through collaborative cross-promotions with like-minded companies or accounts. To do this, you need to independently make arrangements with another company or account that shares a similar audience but isn't a direct competitor. You should arrange to promote their product or account to your audience in exchange for them doing the same in return. If done properly, this can get some new eyes on your brand and allow you to share something of value with your audience – another brand they'll love! You must be very selective in who you partner with because, if done poorly, this will feel like a cheap marketing tactic that will alienate your audience.

If you want to be more aggressive in building your audience, you can explore doing some giveaways. Giveaways can be done in a number of ways but the idea is always the same – offer the chance to win a compelling prize for everyone who performs a certain action(s). The action you require to enter will vary based on the goal of the giveaway, but the most commonly requested actions are: Follow the account hosting the giveaway, tag a friend (or three) within the comment section of the post about the giveaway, share the giveaway by posting about it, or a combination of these. By completing the required actions, the participant has entered the giveaway and now has a chance to win the prize. You can take this a step further by partnering with other brands and requiring participants to follow every account involved to enter the contest. This helps get your message out to a much wider audience that you may otherwise not be able to reach. You can start to see how this can create some virality and yield a ton of followers for a relatively low cost. Even if you give away an expensive prize, the cost often pales in comparison to the cost of reaching that number of people in another way. However, this tactic comes with some major downsides. Giveaways tend to attract a low-quality audience who is more interested in free stuff than they are in your product or brand. The people who are willing to spend their time and effort for a long shot at winning some freebies probably have very little overlap with your core audience. You will most likely attract a bunch of followers who don't ever plan to purchase your product and ultimately don't engage with your posts. This causes low engagement rates which, in turn, cause the social media platform to reduce your content distribution rate to your audience. In the long run, this aggressive strategy may cause more detriment than benefit because the resulting poor distribution rates severely hamper your ability to reach the followers who do care about your brand.

If you decide that giveaways are a good method to grow your following, you need to be sure to adhere to all applicable laws and the social media platform's rules to ensure things go smoothly. Failing to abide by their rules can get your account suspended or terminated. Instagram, for example, requires that you: Clearly state that your contest is not associated with Instagram, include the name of the hosting company, clearly list the contest date/time and time zone, include detailed participation instructions, guidelines, and any limitations (age, location, etc.), state how and when winners will be chosen and announced, and share all details on how prizes should be claimed and delivered. These rules change from time to time, so be sure to check out the platforms latest rules on contests before you get started.

There is one more tactic for instantly building a following that is commonly used by inexperienced entrepreneurs – buying followers. A quick Google search will turn up dozens of offers to sell you thousands of "real and active" followers for a very low price. This can be tempting when just starting out, but it's a terrible idea. All of those followers are bots and they will increase your follower count but they'll never interact with anything you post. Your engagement rates will be terrible, content distribution rates will plummet, and your account will essentially be useless for its entire lifespan. Additionally, you will never be able to build look-alike audiences off your social following or effectively boost a post. What good would it do to boost content to a bunch of bots? Buying followers is a common misstep that should be avoided at all costs.

As you build your audience, you need to serve up a consistent stream of content to keep them engaged. As mentioned earlier, your content should aim to provide some value to your audience. "Value" doesn't have to come in the form of useful information or discounts. People find value in all sorts of content ranging from funny memes to dietary advice. You can even create value by just building a sense of belonging for your followers. Some of the most successful commercial social media accounts do only this and their followers love them for it. Check out @slimjim (yes, the meat stick company) for a shining example of this type of account. They refer to themselves as a "gang" and often tout the tagline "We stand together." Every post involves a slew of inside jokes that only loyal "gang members" will understand. They have done a fantastic job of building a community and creating a sense of belonging for anyone willing to put in the effort to join and understand the "gang." As of this writing, they've amassed over 1.3 million followers and their engagement is extraordinary. They rarely pitch their actual product, but you can imagine that this campaign has had a significant impact on overall sales because they consistently engage a large number of people by providing value, albeit unorthodox value.

Another goal of your social media content should be communicating the values of your brand to followers and potential customers. This doesn't mean you need to list out your values in a post – you probably shouldn't do that. This means that everything you post should be a reflection of the brand you want your customers to perceive. If you make and sell novelty ugly Christmas sweaters, you might post funny memes, unusual alcoholic drink recipes, and video snippets of your customers going a little too hard at their family Christmas parties. This type of content communicates the values of this particular brand. However, if you make and sell lightweight bulletproof vests for law enforcement professionals, you might want to take a more serious approach to your content. This brand will need to communicate vastly different values, so memes may not be the trick. Remember, everything you post is a direct reflection of your brand. Customers will notice, consciously or subconsciously, all the tiny details that collectively signal whether or not your brand is for them.

While you shouldn't constantly post shameless product promotions on your social media accounts, it is important that you monetize these channels to make the effort worthwhile. Don't be afraid to tout new product launches, sales, or special offers for your followers. You can even highlight new uses for your product or explain little-known features. Posts of this sort promote your product while providing value to your audience.

In addition to managing a consistent stream of great content, you also need to pay attention to the social aspect of social media. To maximize engagement you should encourage comments, likes, and direct messages from your followers. Make sure you respond quickly and engage thoroughly when a follower gives you the opportunity. Others will see that they can have an actual interaction with your brand and they will be more likely to engage as well. This is a virtuous cycle that greatly enhances your engagement rates and, subsequently, your content distribution rates. You should also consider regularly taking the time to proactively engage with other accounts. Social media is intended to be a two-way street, so the platforms will often reward those who make proactive efforts to connect with others. This process will also increase total activity on your account and naturally improve your engagement rate over time.

Proper management of organic social media for your business will occupy a lot of time and energy. As always, there are hundreds of agencies that would be happy to help. If you choose to outsource organic social media, be sure to clearly and frequently communicate the type of content and values you want to portray to your audience. Provide consistent, direct, and honest feedback about every aspect of the content they're producing. Ensure all comments and direct messages are replied in a timely and on-brand manner. Also ensure that the tactics they're using to build your following won't have a detrimental long-term effect on your business.

10.10: RETAIL PLACEMENT AS A MARKETING STRATEGY

Not every product can find success with these direct-to-consumer digital marketing techniques. When selling a very low-cost product ($15 or less) it can be difficult to find enough budget to run a profitable digital advertising campaign. You only have a few dollars to spend on ads before you've entirely eliminated any profits. Other products might sell well in person but don't convert online. Certain impulse items, like snacks for example, often just sell better in stores where the customer can take possession of the item immediately. This is where retail placement becomes a critical part of the marketing strategy.

Retail placement isn't only effective for impulse items. Many products and brands can benefit from being on the shelves of trusted stores. If structured and managed properly, retail can provide a great source of revenue and, as importantly, visibility for your product. Every customer walking through the store has the opportunity to see and become aware of your product. Stores are also very selective about the products they choose to sell, so landing on the shelf at a trusted retailer can act as a stamp of approval in the minds of consumers. This immediately improves consumer trust in your product.

While many consider physical retail to be a dying industry, there are still hundreds of thousands of flourishing stores with paying customers walking their aisles every day. This represents a significant opportunity for the right products. However, not every product is suitable for physical retail. Things that sell well online or on Kickstarter don't necessarily sell well in a physical store.

Products that succeed at retail are simple. They do one thing and they do it well. A great example of this is the Scrub Daddy sponge. The product story is simple and the customer understands it at a glance. On the other end of the spectrum, do-all products like the "Travel Jacket with 25 Features" can do very well on Kickstarter but don't stand a chance at retail. These products require too much customer education to sell. They must be accompanied by a detailed video or long writeup. If you can't tell your product story and demonstrate its value in 3 seconds or less, it probably isn't suited for retail.

Retail-ready products must be priced somewhat competitively. There is still room for premium products and brands at common retail, but not ultra-premium. As an example, you could potentially sell a $600 spatula that was machined from a solid block of stainless steel on the internet, but this would never work at retail. Pricing needs to be align with the expectations of the average consumer walking through a specific store. There are a few exceptions like high-fashion brands that sell only at select high-end retailers, but the product pricing still aligns with what shoppers expect to see in a that store.

Your product packaging must also be retail-ready. This means the packaging must be able to hang on a peg hook or sit on a shelf. It must protect your product and simultaneously display it in an appealing way to garner sales. It should also reduce theft and contain the necessary markings to ensure quick checkout.

If your product fits this description, perhaps you should consider physical retail as one of the primary marketing strategies for your product. We'll cover all the details of selling product through wholesale channels in Chapter 12.

CHAPTER 11:

MAXIMIZING SALES

At this point you're driving traffic to your site and starting to make some sales. Now it's time to maximize those sales by refining your website, improving your customer experience, and potentially adding new sales channels like Amazon.com.

As you're refining your website, it's important to understand that there are only three fundamental means to increase the gross revenue generated by an online store: Increase traffic, improve your conversion rate, or increase your average order value. There are thousands of tactics you can implement to influence these key metrics, but these three are the only fundamental levers for improving the top-line revenue generated by your website. Chapter 10 was all about increasing traffic to your website, so we've already covered the first of the three levers in detail. The next lever involves improving your conversion rate.

11.1: IMPROVING CONVERSION RATE

You should strive to maximize the number of website visitors who make a purchase before they leave your site.

If you can go from a 1% conversion rate to a 2% conversion rate, you will literally double the gross revenue generated by your website!

Most branded product websites (not stores that sell many brands of products) have a conversion rate between 1% and 3%. Some exceptional brands can achieve significantly higher conversion rates, but those are few and far between. Incremental improvements to your conversion rate can make an enormous difference to your gross revenue and profitability over time, and they often cost nothing to implement.

First, you need to follow a few fundamental best-practices to ensure that you aren't negatively impacting your conversion rate right off the bat. Most of these fundamentals were covered in detail within the SEO section in Chapter 10, but they're equally important here. Website load speed is critical for maintaining a decent conversion rate. People will leave your site if they have to wait on pages to load. Your site also needs to be built using a responsive template so it adapts seamlessly to mobile traffic. With over half of web traffic coming through mobile devices, you simply cannot afford to ignore the mobile shopper. You also need to ensure your site is easy to navigate. Keep it simple and try to minimize the number of clicks it takes for customers to find the right product and finish checkout. Every extra click in the process will reduce your conversion rate.

Once you have a handle on the absolute basics, you should start to look at other factors that impact conversion rate. Your website must elicit trust in order for shoppers to make a purchase. Try to take an impartial look at the content on your website. Do you have spelling mistakes and low-quality images? These mistakes signal a lack of professionalism and often scare away interested customers. Do you have enough information and photo content to adequately answer any questions or concerns your customer may have? If they have an unanswered concern about your product but your competitor clearly addressed this same concern, you may lose the sale. These are simple issues to address that can make a huge difference over time.

Your shipping, returns, payment, and customer service policies can all have a major impact on your conversion rate as well. When dealing with small companies, customers often don't know what level of service to expect. You need to head off these concerns whenever possible. Clearly list your shipping timeline on the top banner of your website: Ex. "All orders placed by 1PM Eastern ship same day." Consider formulating a free returns policy to reduce risk for the customer. Before you commit to this long-term, you may want to test this policy for a few weeks to see if the extra revenue from the increased conversion rate exceeds the cost of paying for returns. Make checkout and payment as fast and easy as possible. Customers often prefer to pay by PayPal or Amazon Pay instead of entering their credit card information manually. While the processing rates for these services may be a fraction of a percent higher, the increased conversion rate usually makes it worthwhile to have them active. You also need to make it clear that a helpful customer service representative will be available if anything goes wrong. Include your customer service contact information in an obvious place on the website. Also consider including a question/answer section to immediately address the most common concerns customers have when buying from you. You will be surprised at the level of improvement that can be achieved by simply improving and properly advertising your policies and terms of sale.

The next step to refining your website into a conversion machine is A/B testing. There are a number of Shopify apps that allow you to seamlessly serve alternating content to your visitors while measuring and comparing the performance of each variation. This allows you to test different website layouts, product copy, website navigation menus, product pricing, shipping policies (ex. Free shipping vs $5 flat rate), checkout flows, and nearly anything else you might want to compare and refine. Some changes, like switching to free shipping for example, might produce enormous improvements to your conversion rate. Others might be more marginal but still meaningful. If your website is grossing 1 million dollars per year with a 1% conversion rate and you manage to squeeze out an additional .1% through A/B testing, you earned an additional $100,000 with very little added expense. Achieving incremental gains like a .1% improvement is very achievable through A/B testing and will prove to be extremely worthwhile if you put in the effort.

To some degree, A/B testing can be done without any third-party applications or software. The simplest version of A/B testing is to make an alternating change each day for a week or two and see which version performs best. This method can be useful but it has some inherent flaws. Traffic rates to online sites fluctuate, conversion rates change throughout the week, and other outside factors can impact your sales and conversion rate from day to day. You also have to track the time of all the changes and crunch the numbers manually. This system can be insightful, but it's more accurate and useful to use an app or service that will serve the variations to alternating customers and compare the data for you. There are a number of these apps and services available. Some are extremely powerful but costly, while others have fairly limited capabilities and only cost a few dollars per month. If you're just starting out, you can probably make gains with one of the low-cost apps offered in the Shopify app store. When you're ready to get more serious about A/B testing, a service called VWO (VWO.com) offers an excellent balance of capability and price.

11.2: INCREASING AVERAGE ORDER VALUE (AOV)

The third and final lever for augmenting the revenue generated by your website is increasing average order value (AOV). AOV is the total dollar value of orders divided by the number of orders. If you make $1,000 in sales through 10 separate orders, your AOV is $100. Now, what if you can drive that AOV up to $110 instead? Suddenly your $1 million/year website is producing $1,100,000 in gross revenue.

There are a few common methods for increasing your average order value. The first and easiest method is simply raising your price. Will your conversion rate go down if you raise your price by 10%? It's probably worth A/B testing because, often times, the answer is no. It's actually not uncommon to see an improvement in conversion rate when you raise your price because it can add perceived value to your offering and differentiate you from the competition. Another popular method for increasing AOV is through the use of upsell apps or add-on item apps. These plugins allow you to offer customers the opportunity to upgrade to a better version or add an additional item at a discount, right before checkout. It's surprising how many people will impulsively spend a little more for a discounted upgrade or an extra item when directly offered. Multi-packs work in a similar way and don't require any third-party plugins or software. Simply set up a 2-pack or a 6-pack as a separate item in Shopify and offer a slight discount when customers buy larger quantities. You will realize savings on the cost of shipping, fulfillment, and customer acquisition, so the slight discount makes sense. Pass some of the savings on to the customer and keep the rest. It is not unusual for a website to realize a 10% or greater increase in AOV through the use of these tactics.

The apps required to execute these tactics are readily available in the Shopify app store and the cost varies with app capability and the amount of traffic your site receives. Many upsell apps are free for stores with relatively low traffic volumes and most come with a free trial period at minimum. Honeycomb Upsell Funnels is one example that offers a good balance of price and capability.

11.3: THE POWER OF INCREMENTAL IMPROVEMENT

Never underestimate the power of incremental improvements. If you were doing $1 million in annual sales with a 1% conversion rate and a $100 AOV, the new $110 AOV will generate an additional $100,000 of revenue for your site. If you pair this incremental improvement with the .1% improvement to your conversion rate, you get a total revenue of $1,210,000. That's top-line revenue growth of 21% achieved through only incremental improvements. Now let's look at how this impacts the bottom line of your profit and loss statement. It's very expensive to drive more traffic to your site, but that's not how you achieved these gains. Instead, you made better use of the traffic you were already receiving. It typically costs very little to make improvements to conversion rate and AOV, so the extra $210,000 you pulled in is nearly all profit! If you were running at a healthy profit level of 15% the prior year, your pre-tax income was $150,000 from your $1 million in sales. With the addition of $210,000 of high-profit incremental income, your pre-tax income is closer to $360,000! The incremental changes used in this example increased profits by 140%!

It's worth noting that there is usually some cost associated with increasing conversion rate and AOV, so the net profit in the example above isn't perfectly accurate. However, the incremental improvement numbers used in the example are extremely realistic and achievable for most product websites. I strongly encourage you to take the time to work on improving these metrics before you spend a lot of money driving new customers to your site.

11.4: AMAZON.COM AND OTHER THIRD-PARTY SALES CHANNELS

Third-party marketplaces can be another great way to increase your business's revenue and increase product awareness. Amazon.com is probably the best-known example of these marketplaces. Amazon is like a hybrid of the direct-to-consumer and wholesale channels. The seller gets to choose what products they list, build product listings (if it's your original product), determine the price, and manage the inventory flow to the platform's warehouse. The platform manages and sorts the product listing for the customer, handles shipping and fulfillment, manages customer service, and attracts qualified traffic to buy the products that are listed on the site. The platform charges some fees in exchange for the value provided. In the case of Amazon, these fees consist of a monthly subscription (currently $39.99), a percentage of the sale (varies by category but often 15%), shipping and fulfillment fees if you use Fulfillment by Amazon services, and any other fees you rack up like advertising costs, promo rebates, or refunded sales. Total fees will vary based on what you're selling, but I find that the cumulative fees typically end up taking 25%-40% off the top when using their fulfillment services. This puts margins somewhere between those of your website sales and those achieved through selling wholesale, further enforcing that this platform is a true hybrid between the two traditional styles of commerce.

There are a few different ways to sell your product through Amazon. One option is "fulfilled by merchant" (FBM) where the seller (you) holds inventory at their own warehouse and ships orders as they are placed. These shipments aren't typically eligible for "Prime" 2-day shipping so they are a much less popular choice among customers. FBM will save some money on fulfillment fees and can be a good option under certain circumstances (shipping large furniture, for example), but it will greatly handicap your sales due to the lack of free Prime shipping. A better option for most sellers is "fulfilled by Amazon," or FBA. This is where a seller sends their inventory to an Amazon warehouse so Amazon can manage the fulfillment and shipment of orders directly. FBA inventory is eligible for Prime shipping and this allows you to offer the same service level as Amazon and other top-tier sellers. The inventory is owned by the seller until it is sold to the customer – Amazon never actually buys or sells the product in this instance. FBA has quickly become the most popular choice for successful sellers on Amazon. Many sellers find that they sell significantly more (as much as 10X in my experience) when they switch from FBM to FBA. You can set up and manage your seller account for FBM or FBA through the Seller Central platform: https://sellercentral. amazon.com/

The third and final way to work with Amazon is through Vendor Central. This is where you develop a traditional wholesale relationship with Amazon and they buy your product to resell on their platform. Unlike FBM or FBA, they control the offer price and the product listings directly in this scenario. Amazon will typically want generous wholesale margins plus backend fees (more on that in chapter 12) for this arrangement. While you can imagine that there could be some serious benefits to having the platform manage and promote your product, the loss of margin and price control may be a difficult pill to swallow in exchange. It's important to note that, unlike FBM or FBA, you can't just sign up for Vendor Central. You must be invited by Amazon directly. Brands are often approached after they show outstanding success selling through FBA, or occasionally at tradeshows. If you do get the offer to join Vendor Central, evaluate the terms closely because you might not want to accept. I, personally, declined the invitation to transition one of my brands to Vendor Central due to the prospective loss of price control and lower margins.

As a product entrepreneur, your experience will be a little different from most other Amazon sellers. You have an original product of your own creation and you care about the quality of the product listings, the reviews, the pricing, and the impact Amazon has on the rest of your business. Most sellers are simply hawking other people's products that they managed to acquire at a discount, and they only care about landing the "buy box" and making the sale. Since your goals are different, your strategies should be different as well. Perhaps the most important thing you will need to do differently is signing up for the Amazon Brand Registry. This is a program where you prove to Amazon that you own the registered trademark for a specific brand and claim the exclusive ability to edit product listings. This prevents other sellers from constantly changing your product listings to fit their own needs and desires. You will need to register your trademark with the USPTO in order to apply for the Amazon Brand Registry.

Product pricing should be another aspect that you handle differently from the general selling community. Most sellers will try to price their product lower than all the other sellers while still making a little money. This helps ensure their offer wins the "buy box." The seller with the most competitive offer (a metric comprised of a combination of factors but mostly influenced by offer price) will win the buy box, meaning that their product is the one that is sold and shipped when the customer buys an item. As a brand owner, you don't want to see your product devalued in this way if you can avoid it. To be successful on sales channels outside Amazon, you must maintain your MSRP on Amazon. This can be very challenging, but it starts with you. Do not offer your product for less on Amazon than it is offered elsewhere, or you will handicap all other sales channels and destroy the sales of your retail partners. Additionally, you should strongly consider limiting or restricting your wholesale accounts from selling on third-party platforms for this exact reason. If twelve different sellers are selling your item, a price war will ensue and your product will quickly become devalued. You must clearly communicate any restrictions around third-party platforms with every wholesale account before you accept their first order. Nearly every account will try to sell your product on third-party platforms if you don't clearly restrict them from doing so.

After you get your product listing up and running, you'll probably want to run some ads to drive traffic to your product. These third-party platforms sort products by relevance and popularity, so you need to put in some effort to get some initial momentum and work your way through the rankings. Just like with SEO, your goal is to get as high as possible in the search rankings for as many relevant search terms as you can. Since there are millions of products available on Amazon, you will probably need to run some ads to get this initial momentum, generate some sales, get product reviews, and ultimately achieve good organic search rankings on the platform. The Amazon ad campaign manager is accessed through Seller Central and it works a lot like Google AdWords. You enter a bid for a keyword and, if your bid and relevance generate the highest ranking, your ad will serve when someone searches that specific keyword. You can access all the ROAS data directly in the Seller Central Campaign Manager. Keep in mind that the data in the campaign manager is measured off the gross sales, but this is deceiving since there are significant platform fees that cut into your gross when selling on a third-party platform. Your actual ROAS will be much lower than shown in the campaign manager once you account for these fees.

Amazon has quickly become one of the largest sales platforms in the world and it can enable your brand to access millions of potential customers that you otherwise may not reach. At the same time, it comes with some downsides that should be seriously considered before you join. The biggest downside is that selling on Amazon will impact your direct web sales and those of your retail partners. Many customers prefer to buy on Amazon so, even if they discover the product elsewhere, they may still go to Amazon to make the purchase. Losing sales to Amazon can make it difficult to measure the actual ROAS of the ads you're running for your own website. Another downside is that the Amazon shopping experience isn't great for educating and building loyal customers. Amazon is optimized to convert, not to browse, learn, or engage. As a seller, you have limited control over the assets you can use to showcase your product and much of your product page will be occupied with similar and competitive products from other brands. You may be doing the work to bring new customers to the product category while Amazon sells them on your competitor's product directly on your product page. Amazon is also the primary place that bottom-feeding copy-cats look for product ideas to replicate. Since there is a category sales ranking on every product, these bottom-feeders can sort categories by the best sellers to see what products are worth ripping off. If you find success on Amazon, you can expect dozens of low-priced knockoffs to hit the market shortly thereafter. One final issue with selling your product on Amazon is that retail partners might be hesitant to carry your product in their store. They know that many customers prefer to buy from Amazon and they also know how difficult it is to maintain MSRP when there are multiple sellers of a given item an Amazon. If they see these potential issues with your product, they may choose to carry something else instead. If you have big plans to approach retail stores, you should take the time to thoroughly evaluate your Amazon strategy before you commit.

None of these downsides are inherently deal-breakers. Every product business has different needs and priorities, so it's up to you to weigh the pros and cons to make an educated decision around third-party platforms. You might even come up with some clever strategies to make third-party platforms work entirely in your favor. Consider pricing your product slightly higher on these platforms than elsewhere (if they'll let you). Also consider making yourself the only party authorized to sell your product on third-party platforms so you can control the pricing for your retail partners. Alternatively, you can dedicate a single, qualified, trusted partner as the only authorized third-party seller so they can maintain product and pricing integrity on your behalf. The most important thing for a product entrepreneur approaching third-party platforms is to develop a strategy that keeps the entire business in focus, not just sales on that specific platform.

Amazon may be the big name in the space, but there are plenty of other third-party marketplaces out there. Ebay. com, Etsy.com, Walmart.com, HomeDepot.com, WayFair. com, and NewEgg.com are all popular third-party platforms that you could conceivably sell your product through. Most of these have some specialty or market niche that they serve. For example, Etsy is intended for hand-made goods and NewEgg is mostly focused on consumer electronics. It probably isn't worthwhile to place your product on every third-party website that will accept it. They each require some level of maintenance and most will only generate a very small fraction of the sales you can make through Amazon.com. To avoid wasted time and effort, focus only on Amazon and the marketplaces that specialize in your type of product.

Selling on Amazon is an enormous topic and, like several other topics discussed so far, it would require its own book to cover with any level of detail. The goal of this section is to outline the process, benefits, and drawbacks of working with third-party platforms so you can develop a strategy for your business. If you decide to go forward with selling on third-party platforms directly, I recommend you do some additional research before getting started. Amazon provides a wealth of resources to help sellers get started on their platform: https://sell.amazon.com/sell.html. There are also several dedicated books on the topic that will provide a little more insight and detail. Check out *Selling on Amazon for Dummies* by Deniz Olmez. Additionally, there is an enormous amount of information available on forums and e-seller blogs covering nearly any detail you can imagine, and these can all be accessed by typing your question into the Google search bar. As you do your research, constantly check for the date that a particular book or article was written. These platforms evolve quickly so information that is more than a couple of years old is probably outdated. It's also important to remember that most of this information is written from the viewpoint of a normal seller, not a product entrepreneur. Always keep the larger question in mind when making decisions about third-party platforms: "What is best for the overall business?"

As you might expect, there are hundreds of consultants willing to help you manage Amazon and other third-party platforms if you find the task overwhelming. There are a few different business models out there and some won't cost you anything out of pocket if you have a successful product. One common model for Amazon consultants is an exclusive wholesale partnership where the consultant is the only party authorized to sell your product on the platform. They buy product from you at wholesale pricing and resell it on Amazon, keeping the difference. In exchange for the discounted pricing and exclusivity, they do all the work associated with properly managing your brand on the platform (it is a lot of work to do it properly). Other consultants may do the work for a flat monthly rate, a flat rate plus commission, or just a commission on total sales. There is no right or wrong way to structure this partnership; it really depends on your needs and the state of your business. If you choose to work with a consultant, especially in the exclusive partner model, make the partner sign an agreement stating that they will not list the products lower than the MSRP.

As Amazon has grown into the behemoth it is, properly managing a brand on the platform has become increasingly difficult. While it's certainly not necessary, working with a consultant to get things set up and running properly from the start will often pay for itself in the first few months. A good consultant can flatten out the learning curve, helping you avoid common mistakes and maximize sales quickly. As always with consultants, references are critical for sniffing out the good ones.

CHAPTER 12:

SELLING WHOLESALE TO RETAILERS

Placing your product in brick-and-mortar retail stores is a powerful way to gain exposure among millions of potential new customers. It can also be a great revenue source if managed properly. These upsides come with their challenges, though. Once you start working with retailers, your business becomes vastly more complex and difficult to manage. You trade much of your margin in exchange for volume, so efficiency becomes critical. You also have to closely manage your financials and cash flow because retailers expect to pay for items well after they receive them. You will need to build a competent team to make this work at any significant scale, which means hiring and managing people. Along with that comes human resource tasks like payroll taxes, healthcare plans, vacation policies and everything else associated with building a team. You can already see how the decision to sell at retail will totally alter the structure and complexity of your business. This decision should not be taken lightly.

Selling wholesale isn't the right fit for every entrepreneur or every product. Before you make this move, evaluate the goals you have for your business. Do you simply want to generate a nice salary with minimal hassle, or do you want to build the next big thing? Both of these are valid paths, but if the former is your goal then I advise you to stick to online selling only.

Likewise, not every product is suited for brick-and-mortar retail. Retail-ready products typically need to appeal to a pretty wide audience. If a store is going to commit valuable shelf space to a product, they need to be certain that a good percentage of their shoppers will be interested. Extremely niche products are often best kept online. Good retail products also need to be simple. A customer needs to know if they're interested in a single glance made at a walking pace. If you're selling the "Travel Jacket with 25 Features," shoppers will only see a jacket as they give it a once-over. Brick-and-mortar shoppers don't stop at every product to read the box or tag. They don't examine every item with an open mind, hoping they might find something they like. Their eyes are quickly scanning and their brain is editing out everything that doesn't exhibit immediate value. If your product story isn't simple and obvious enough to sell itself at a glance, physical retail may not be the right path.

If you decide to move forward and pursue physical retail placement, it's imperative that you have the proper accounting software setup before you open any wholesale accounts. You will need the ability to create customer accounts, issue invoices, track payments and due dates, send overdue payment reminders, run detailed reports, and a number of other tasks that would be extremely difficult without the proper resources. QuickBooks Online is a great option that will have all the capability you need for years to come. There are other options available, but QuickBooks is typically the go-to platform for small product businesses.

12.1: RETAIL MARGINS, ALLOWANCES, AND TERMS

Retailers provide a lot of value for brands. They bring the product to the customer and the customer to the product. This is an expensive proposition. They have to pay for the valuable real estate in a high traffic area, the building, utilities, the staff for the store, freight for the products, and hundreds of other significant expenses. They also have massive advertising budgets to attract qualified shoppers.

All this value doesn't come cheap for brands. Retailers expect to buy the products they sell at a significant discount so they can still turn a profit despite all these expenses. Retailers expect different margins for different product types and categories (Remember margin from Chapter 1? (price-cost)/price). Retailers might ask for margins as high as 80% in some categories like cell phone cases. Other categories, like flatscreen televisions, may call for only 15% margin to the retailer. Unless your product lands in a category with unusual margins, you should expect to offer your retailers a traditional 50% margin. A 50% margin is also called "keystone," and this means the retailer buys the product for half the price at which they intend to sell it. Large retailers typically have "backend" fees on top of their margin. These are typically 1%-2% fees and discounts that nickel and dime you out of a considerable amount of money.

Backend fees are calculated as a percentage discount from the wholesale price, not from MSRP. Common backend fees include an "advertising allowance" that they're supposed to spend advertising your product. "Return allowances" cover the cost of returned merchandise so they don't have to negotiate return costs with the supplier on an item-by-item basis. "New store allowances" give retailers free inventory to fill out a store whenever they open a new location. This is typically a handful of units per SKU that you provide at no cost. These three fees are the most common, but there are various others you may encounter from time to time. The cumulative total of all fees applied by a major retailer will often score them a discount of 6%-10% off the wholesale cost! This is a significant discount that you need to plan for from the outset. These fees are typically outlined and agreed to during the vendor setup process, so keep a close eye out for them when reviewing your on-boarding paperwork. Small retailers with just few locations don't typically ask for backend fees and allowances.

In addition to expensive fees, you should also expect to offer payment terms (commonly referred to as simply "terms") to your retail partners. Terms define the payment structure and the amount of time an account gets to pay for an order. Terms are intended to help retailers manage cashflow. Their businesses are inventory-heavy and financing all the inventory in advance can be challenging. Terms allow them to sell through some of the inventory before they have to pay for it, making the financial management of a retail store more manageable. Longer terms are more generous to the retailer and they will put much more strain on your business. Typical terms start at 30 days and this is commonly referred to as "net 30." Net 30 means that the full balance is due within 30 days from the invoice date. Net 45 and 60 are also common, but less desirable for your business. Some extremely large retailers will ask for net 90 and beyond. I recommend avoiding these deals unless you have a significant stockpile of cash to fund their inventory that far out.

To incentivize early payment and improve cash flow for the seller, terms will often include a discount for early payment. If you want to offer a 2% discount for payment received within 10 days of invoice while still offering 30 day payment terms, that would be written as follows: 2/10 net 30. Similarly, a 1% discount for payment within 15 days with net terms of 45 days would be: 1/15 net 45. Many retail partners will gladly take a small discount in exchange for early payment. This can be greatly beneficial to a young product company, especially one without significant outside funding.

12.2: SELLING YOUR PRODUCT INTO STORES

With literally tens-of-millions of different products on the market, retail stores have to be extremely selective about what they carry. Even the largest stores can only fit around 100,000 discreet SKUs. There simply isn't room to carry everything and shelf space is expensive. Retailers need to make the most possible money per square foot to cover their cost of doing business.

The people who decide what a retail store will carry are called "buyers" (or sometimes "merchants"). Buyers are typically divided by category and it's their job to ensure the sales and profitability of that category are strong. Their job performance is typically evaluated on sell-through, inventory holdings, and gross margin. Even an incremental improvement in these metrics is seen as a great success, so buyers don't often take big risks. This conservative mindset can make it difficult for new products to make the cut. Getting retail placement doesn't happen overnight. It's a long journey that starts with building relationships with store buyers. The first step to building a relationship is making contact.

Buyers for mom-and-pop stores with a single location often work in the store itself. It's common for the buyer role to be just one of many hats worn by the owner or a single employee of a small store. You can often reach the buyer by simply walking in and asking to speak to the buyer of your product category. For a more professional approach, you can ask for their email address and try to set up an appointment time instead. For stores that aren't local to you, the contact information on the website of a small store will often go directly to the owner/buyer.

Buyers for large chain stores are much harder to reach. They typically work at the corporate headquarters rather than the actual store locations. More often than not, nobody at the store locations has any influence at all over what products the store carries. It's futile to walk into a Target store and ask to speak to a category buyer. Instead, you might consider doing some research on LinkedIn to see if you can determine the proper contact. Send a casual offer to connect with a little information on your product. If you get a response, offer to send out a sample or see if they're willing to set up an appointment at an upcoming tradeshow. Even better, see if you can visit their headquarters to pitch your product and discuss store placement.

Before you begin pitching your product to buyers, you need to get some basic documentation together. Develop a product sales sheet or catalog with all the information a buyer might need to know about your product. This should include the product name, an image, the SKU, dimensions, features, specs, a product description, and the MSRP. You should also have a price sheet containing your wholesale pricing for each item you plan to pitch. Offer to send samples alongside this documentation if you can do so at a reasonable cost. Your goal is to make it as easy as possible for a buyer to say "yes." Put all the necessary information in one place to make it simple for them to add your product to their assortment.

Cold-calling store buyers is a tough, slow way to build a presence at retail. If you're serious about getting store placement, you should consider exhibiting at a tradeshow. Tradeshows can be a great place to meet buyers and present your product. Most industries have their own shows (hardware, outdoor, gift, fashion, surf, food, etc.) and you can usually find these shows with a quick Google search. Do your research in advance to make sure your product fits the theme of the show. There's nothing worse than spending a bunch of money to exhibit at a show where you just don't belong. If you have the opportunity, attend the show once before you exhibit there. You need to have a good understanding of the amount of traffic on the floor, the type and scale of booth that other companies bring, and who else will be exhibiting. These factors vary greatly from show to show, so you need to understand what you're up against.

Tradeshows are most effective if you can set up appointments with specific buyers in advance. There are still a lot of benefits to showing up and trying to build relationships from the available foot traffic, but pre-booked appointments are the name of the game. This can be difficult for a new brand without existing relationships or buyer contacts, so you may have to pay your dues for the first few years. Use those early shows to make connections and acquire contacts. Follow up with the contacts afterwards and continue to build the relationship. When the next show approaches, try to schedule appointments in advance with the contacts you've made at prior shows. After every show, follow up with every buyer who showed interest in your product. More sales are typically made in the follow-up than at the show itself.

When approaching buyers, it's important to understand their needs and limitations. These buyers typically work on seasonal cycles to ensure their offering aligns with what customers will be looking for. Different industries "reset" at different intervals. Many industries reset twice per year, grouping spring and summer together, and fall and winter. Other industries, like apparel, work on 4 season cycles. The buyers for major stores typically plan their assortments seven to twelve months in advance. This means that you're often pitching your product in May to potentially land on shelves the following spring. Their purchasing budget aligns with these cycles as well. The available purchasing budget is often referred to as a buyer's "open-to-buy dollars." To get your product included in their assortment, you need to have your product in their hands while they still have open-to-buy dollars available. Small retailers often follow a similar cycle, but they will occasionally pick up some SKUs mid-season. They often have more flexibility than the majors.

In addition to having budget, buyers also need to have space for your product. Available space is commonly referred to as "white space." If a buyer has no white space available, they will have to drop another product to include yours in their assortment. It can be difficult to convince them to swap an existing SKU for a new one unless they have some real under-performers in their lineup.

Even if all these stars align, your product still might not get assorted. Assorting a product from a young company presents a significant risk for a buyer. They don't know for certain that you'll be able to live up to expectations as a supplier. You could have quality issues, or challenges keeping product in stock. You might even go out of business entirely. These are common occurrences with young companies and all of these scenarios leave retailers losing money from the empty peg hooks in their store.

If you only plan to supply one or two items to a retailer, this can be a hurdle as well. Every supplier they add has to be set up in their system and managed independently. It saves buyers a lot of time and energy if they work with fewer partners who each supply a large number of items. Vendor setup with a major retailer can take 6 months or more, so it's a considerable amount of work to add new ones. This can cause a buyer to choose a less exciting product from an existing supplier instead of yours.

Smaller stores may not share these concerns. Their new vendor setup process often takes just a few minutes and they can pivot more readily if you have supply issues. This makes mon-and-pop shops an ideal starting point for inexperienced product entrepreneurs looking to place their product at retail.

Buyers are busy and they get solicited by product companies all day every day. It can take years of work to build a relationship, demonstrate value, and work your way onto the shelves of a major retailer. Don't get discouraged by the long process. Many successful brands struggle to break into major retailers initially, only to find great success once they do. If you don't want to wait, the use of experienced reps and distributors can greatly shorten your path to success, but they come at a cost. We'll discuss these options in detail later in this chapter.

12.3: TRADESHOWS

Tradeshows are one of the most effective ways to meet buyers and sell into retail stores. These shows are extremely expensive for exhibitors. Floor space is typically $20 to $50 per square foot, meaning that a tiny 10x10 foot booth will cost you $2,000 to $5,000. Medium-sized booths like a 30x20 footer can run $12,000 to $30,000. This doesn't include all the other expenses associated with the tradeshow circuit.

You need to have a physical booth, which will often cost tens-of-thousands of dollars for a nice one. You have freight and drayage to the convention center. Drayage is the fee the labor unions charge to move your freight from the loading dock of the convention center to your booth location and back. You can expect $1,000 or more for freight and a similar amount for drayage of a small to medium sized booth. You also need a day or two to set up your booth and trained employees to staff the booth during the show. Most shows won't be local to you, so you should also expect to incur significant travel expenses for you and your staff. All in all, tradeshows cost a small fortune.

There are a few tricks to save a little money on tradeshows. If you're handy and can build your own booth, the savings there are significant. You can also hire the tradeshow labor union to build you a single-use booth on-site, which is usually cheaper than building and shipping a permanent booth if you don't plan to do a lot of shows. If your booth is lightweight, you can drive it to the show and hand-carry it inside piece by piece. Most shows and associated labor unions do not allow you to use wheeled carts and they restrict hand-carry of items over a certain weight. If you need to ship your booth to the show, use a service like Exhibit Transfer Inc. to book your freight. They have highly negotiated rates with carriers and understand the logistics of each show, making it easy to manage your fright to and from destination. You can often get a discount on floor space by signing up early, or by becoming a member of the association that puts on the show. The membership fees are often less than the booth savings, saving you as much as a few thousand dollars. The combined savings of these tricks will be significant.

Every tradeshow will provide an exhibitor guide well in advance of the show. You need to review this guide in detail to ensure you know all the rules during setup, during the show, and during teardown. This guide will also outline all of the shipping and labeling requirements for your freight. The labor unions that run these shows are typically pretty unforgiving and they will charge you an arm and a leg for any rules you break or any mistakes you might make along the way.

Every show is a little different. Some require stripped-down booths with little flair to ensure business remains the primary focus. These are typically order writing shows, meaning that buyers show up with a budget in mind and plan to place orders at the show. You need to be prepared with catalogs, price sheets, new dealer application forms, and order sheets so you can take advantage of this buying environment. Other shows, especially the larger ones, have evolved into more of a PR and entertainment event. The booths are huge and extravagant. Brands might have celebrities hanging out in their booth to attract a crowd. Booths are full of exotic cars, models, and free booze. Business still gets done at these shows, but it's hardly the focus. Pre-booked appointments with media and buyers are key at these shows. These can also present a good networking opportunity to collect contacts for the future. In my experience, you rarely walk away with many written orders from these larger shows. Instead, the goal is to show your product line for the next relevant season and then get the order later through follow-up. It's very important that you understand the show that you'll be attending so you can plan and set your expectations accordingly.

12.4: WHOLESALE SETUP AND ORDERING PROCESS – WHAT TO EXPECT

Setting up a wholesale account with a small store is relatively simple. Once both parties are ready to move forward, the brand should send over a new dealer application for the store to complete. This form should have fields for the new dealer's basic information including business name, website, billing address, and phone number. It should also request their accounts payable information including the accounting contact name, email address, and phone number. Additionally, the form should have fields to collect their shipping address, warehouse contact details including phone and email, preferred shipping carrier and the associated account number, plus any special shipping instructions. This completed form should have all the information you need to set up a new dealer in your system, ship them product, and properly bill their account.

If the new account wants terms (most will), you should include a credit application. This application should request the new dealer's DUNS number (Dun and Bradstreet Number) and three trade references. The DUNS number is managed by Dun and Bradstreet who is essentially the credit reporting agency for businesses. Their database is incomplete for very small companies like single-store retail shops so it's much more useful when you're evaluating large corporations. It's also pricey to access the data so this service may not be worthwhile for you. Trade references, on the other hand, are free and can be quite telling. Contact the references provided before you extend terms. Often these references will tell you honestly whether the account in question has any history of late or incomplete payment. You should think twice about extending terms to anyone whose trade references are less-than-excellent. You can still work with accounts who don't qualify for terms by requiring that they pay in full prior to shipping their order.

Once you've collected all the necessary information and set the customer up in your system (most likely QuickBooks), they can send a purchase order (commonly called a "PO") committing to buy the listed goods. Their purchase order should clearly state the product they intend to order, the quantity, and the price. You will, in exchange, send an invoice for the ordered goods. This invoice should be generated by your accounting software. If the dealer who issued the PO has been approved for terms, you're ready to ship their order. If pre-payment is required, you will want to wait on that payment to process before you arrange shipment. After you ship the order, the account with terms should send payment for the order within the specified payment window. However, it doesn't always work this way. You should get in the habit of sending reminders to accounts that are overdue on their payments. Many busy store owners fail to keep track of payments due, so a simple reminder when they are overdue is often enough to get the bill paid and complete the transaction.

Large retailers are a whole different animal. While the milestones of the process are similar, there are many more steps involved.

Larger retail chains will often have a pre-prepared vendor guide or a dedicated website containing all the necessary resources to on-board a new supplier. This guide or site will contain all the information you would normally collect through your new dealer application form, and more. Large retailers will typically send over a Seller Agreement outlining the terms of the relationship. This may be accompanied by a Payment and Allowance Agreement outlining those details as well. These documents must be signed and returned, acknowledging that you know and understand the terms of the partnership.

They will also send a Routing Guide with detailed instructions on how to arrange shipments to their distribution center (commonly called a "DC"). These guides can sometimes approach 200 pages in length and it's important that you understand your responsibilities as a supplier. You will receive a "chargeback" whenever you make a mistake shipping to a major retailer's distribution center. A chargeback is a penalty assessed to the shipper to cover the cost of the mistake. These can range from $30 to $200 and you want to avoid them like the plague. Chargebacks are typically outlined in the on-boarding paperwork you receive from the dealer.

Special labels are required for shipments going to the DC of a large retailer. These labels are designed to be read by automatic scanners on conveyor systems and they ensure the goods flow smoothly through the DC. Generating these labels requires the use of a technology called Electronic Data Interchange, or EDI. EDI is basically a system that enables different databases to exchange information using a standardized language. Whichever EDI system you choose to implement within your business will enable you to seamlessly transfer information and shipment data to the retailer. In addition to creating shipping labels, EDI is used to transmit POs, send invoices, submit order changes, transmit tracking information, and generally automate common communication between the retailer and supplier. As a small company, you will want to use a third-party cloud-based EDI service provider for your EDI needs. There are a whole host of these suppliers out there, each with a slightly different offering that achieves same thing. The cheaper options are cheap for a reason. They require a lot of manual input and can be quite a hassle to deal with. The premium options will automate and streamline your processes significantly, but they can cost ten times more. The prices range from $40 per month to $400 per month to get started. There is typically an extra monthly fee for every partner you connect with.

Large retailers will send you questionnaires about your business to complete and return, rather than vice versa. They use this information to set up your vendor account and send you payments. Once your company is set up in their system, they need to set up your SKUs. They will usually send over an article creation document containing the names of the items the plan to carry. You enter all the remaining details about your products and send this completed document back to them. This information is used to populate their backend systems and often their website product listings.

Similar to small dealers, large retailers will place their orders using a purchase order, but theirs will be transmitted by EDI rather than email. Instead of emailing back to let them know the order was received, you will respond by sending a Purchase Order Acknowledgement via EDI to confirm you have accepted the order. When it comes time to ship the order, you will transmit an Advance Ship Notice (ASN) via EDI. The ASN contains important information to identify the shipment and its contents. The invoice is then transmitted by EDI after the order has shipped. This probably sounds like gibberish now, but it will make sense once you start to on-board an EDI provider and work your way through the setup process.

12.5: RETAIL SELL-THROUGH AND REPORTING

Getting on the shelves is just half the battle. The real challenge is selling through. Sell-through is the rate at which your product is purchased in the store. If sell-through isn't strong your product will eventually get cut. It's important that you work with your buyer to merchandise your product in a compelling way that drives sales. You should also check the sell-through data for your products regularly so you can head off any potential issues. Most major retailers will offer a portal for you to regularly check your sales data. These portals can be quite confusing because they use so many cryptic acronyms. It's nearly impossible to find the meaning of these acronyms online and it's embarrassing to ask your buyer what they mean because that shows them that you don't know what you're doing! To save you the trouble and embarrassment, I've compiled a list of the various acronyms you'll encounter on a sell-through report below. Some of these seem obvious when seen individually with the meaning written beside them, but they get much more confusing when combined into a cryptic-seeming code like TY WTD UNITS 4WK AVG SLS, which means "this year, week to date, units, 4 week average sales." Knowing these acronyms is a must to make heads or tails of these sell-through reports.

AVG: Average

GM%: Gross Margin expressed as a percentage

GM: Gross Margin

OH: On Hand

OO: On Order

RTL: Retail

SLS: Sales

ST%: Sell-Through Percentage

TO: Turnover

TY: This Year

VAR: Variance

WK: Week

WOS: Weeks Of Supply

WTD: Week To Date

YTD: Year To Date

12.6: DISTRIBUTORS AND SALES REPS

Making contact and building relationships with buyers can take years. If you'd like to speed up the process at the expense of some margin, you should look into using a distributor. Distributors carry products from many brands and they act as a middle man between brands and retailers. They buy product in bulk from a brand, warehouse it, and distribute it to stores as it's ordered. A good distributor should have a comprehensive sales team with pre-existing relationships with the proper category buyer at nearly every store you want to be in. They should already be setup as a vendor in these retailer's systems. They should also fully understand each account's routing guide and have a good history of consistent fulfillment.

Distributors can often get your product placed on retail shelves faster because they circumvent many of the concerns buyers have about working with young brands directly. When working with a distributor, buyers don't have to on-board a new supplier to add new products to their assortment. They can place one order for hundreds of items, saving themselves time. They know the distributor is a reliable supplier who probably isn't going out of business soon. Distributors take away much of the risk and the hassle, and this can be appealing to buyers.

Because of their existing relationships, distributors can often get your product in front of buyers at the very next reset meeting. If you chose your distributor well, they should already be selling other products to the relevant category buyer. This means they probably meet with the buyer at least twice a year to plan the future assortment. If a good distributor picks up your product, it will get pitched to the right person in the next meeting cycle. This alone can save you several years that it often takes to get your first meeting with a category buyer at a major retail chain.

As you probably suspect, this service doesn't come cheap. Distributors can provide a lot of value but they take a healthy margin for their efforts. This margin varies by product category, but 30% is not uncommon for general consumer products. Remember that they still have to offer significant margin to the retailer, so this 30% is taken off the wholesale price. If your item's MSRP is $100, you can expect to sell it to a distributor for around $35 (The math: $100 x .5 = $50. $50 x .7 = $35. We multiply by .7 because that's your keep after you give the distributor 30%, or .3). Since distributors provide a lot of convenience for buyers as well, they can sometimes negotiate placement for a slightly lower margin to the retailer. If they can convince the buyer to accept a 40% margin instead of 50%, you would be selling the $100 item to the distributor for $42. None of these calculations include any backend fees from the retailer, which will further cut into your margin.

Assuming you used the pricing model we discussed in Chapter 1, you will still be able to pull a 25%-40% margin for yourself when working with a distributor. This isn't too bad if you consider that you don't have to employ your own sales team, exhibit at expensive tradeshows, or manage the inventory and sales terms associated with selling to retail.

Working with a good distributor can greatly simplify your life as a product entrepreneur.

As with everything in this business, distributors come with their own healthy dose of downsides. First and foremost, you're losing significant margin when you sell through a distributor. The services they provide may or may not be worth the cost to you. Second, they're building the relationships with stores and buyers, not you. After working with a distributor, you still won't have the contacts and experience necessary to sell directly to the store in the future, nor will you be setup as a supplier in their system. Third, you have little control over your product pricing and where it's sold. You rely entirely on the distributor to maintain pricing integrity and they may not care about it nearly as much as you do. Additionally, you can expect a number of their accounts to sell on third-party platforms like Amazon.com. This takes away your ability to own and properly manage the sale of your product on those platforms. Fourth, distributors typically negotiate exclusive rights to your product within a specific territory (there are usually a few exceptions like your own website and third-party platforms). If they have the exclusive right to sell your product in a critical territory like the U.S. and they don't put in the effort to do a good job, you're trapped with low sales in a key region for the duration of the contract.

These downsides may or may not seem like a big deal to you. Every entrepreneur weighs them differently and it should really depend on the goals you have for your business. If you are looking to build a hands-off machine that generates a solid income, a distributor is probably the way to go. If you want to build your own team and run a proper company with massive growth potential, you might want to sell directly to retail instead.

Distributors can be particularly useful in foreign countries where you aren't able or ready to build a proper sales and distribution network. International distributors work a lot like domestic distributors except they typically get exclusive rights to a specific country or set of countries. It's fairly common for young brands to use international distributors to cover every territory outside their home country, and this isn't a bad practice. International distributors can quickly expand your reach and grow your market with minimal effort.

If you manufacture your product overseas, you will probably want to arrange shipments to international distributors directly from the factory. This can result in considerable savings by only paying freight and duties once. If you're an American company who manufactures in China and sells to a distributor in Brazil, you will pay fright and duties twice if you import to your U.S. warehouse before you ship and import to Brazil. You can carve out much better margins if you negotiate FOB terms at the port nearest your factory. Experienced international distributors will expect FOB terms and they should already be well versed in the import process.

As always, references are critical when choosing a domestic or international distributor. You should try to find a distributor who has years of experience distributing similar products in your exact industry. This will ensure the distributor has the proper relationships and capabilities to manage your brand well. You can often find distributors exhibiting at tradeshows. They're typically the ones showcasing products from many different brands in their booth. Don't hesitate to approach someone in their booth and ask for the proper contact to send over some information on your product.

For those who decide to approach retail without a distributor, you might want to consider building out a team of sales reps instead. Sales reps are typically independent contractors who work with a handful of different brands at once. They are usually paid only commission on the sales generated in their territory. Reps work a specific region (usually a handful of states in the U.S.) and they often require exclusive rights to all accounts within their territory. In exchange, they act like your own regional sales force. A good rep will have pre-existing relationships with the buyers at the potential accounts within their territory. They'll arrange meetings and do their best to sell your product into every store they can. They'll visit the stores in their territory on occasion, checking to see how your product looks on the shelf and tidying things up if needed. They'll help you strategize, build, and roll out compelling wholesale programs to improve sell-through and brand visibility. They can be especially critical in helping you reach all the independent specialty stores that you would otherwise never reach.

Reps are significantly different from distributors. They don't carry any inventory and they aren't set up as suppliers with any retailers. Your company will be set up as the supplier and you will be responsible for inventory management, shipping, and logistics to the accounts they bring on. The reps are simply your sales team, working to get your product on the shelves of desirable accounts. When working with reps, you still get final say over who you ship to. You can continue to own and manage third-party platforms in the way you like. You also lose significantly less margin since they tend to cost less than a distributor. Building a team of quality reps is not easy. They are judicious about the brands and products they will represent. However, if you're able to get good reps on board, they can be a great balance between a distributor and doing everything yourself.

Rep commission varies by industry and volume. Large companies that move a lot of volume can pay a significantly lower commission percentage than smaller companies who sell less. When you're starting out, you should expect to pay upwards of 10% commission for a good rep in many industries. This commission is calculated from the price at which they sell the product, typically wholesale.

Good reps or rep agencies can be difficult to find. If you have contacts at other companies within your industry, ask around to see if anyone knows of a good rep agency for a given territory. Tradeshows can also be a good place to start your search. Most reps attend the relevant industry tradeshows so they're there if you can find them. If you have relationships with any retail buyers, you can also ask them if they know of any good reps or rep agencies in the area. Retail buyers should hear from all the good regional reps on a regular basis, so they can be a great source of information on this topic.

12.7: DROP SHIPPING

Drop shipping is when one company sells a product without ever owning or possessing it, and another company ships it directly to the purchaser for a portion of the proceeds from the sale. Some online stores specialize in drop shipping. They advertise, attract customers and make the sale, but they don't hold any inventory or ship any orders. Instead, they send a shipping order to the product brand who then ships the product to the customer. The store then sends a portion of the purchase proceeds to the brand in exchange for the product and fulfillment services.

Drop shipping was all the rage a decade ago. It's a great deal for the store and a terrible deal for the product brand in most circumstances. The store makes a cut of the profits from the sale without investing in inventory, warehousing, or shipping the product. The brand, on the other hand, gets a smaller cut of the sale while financing all the inventory, taking all the risk, and doing all the work.

These days, drop shipping is mostly dead. There are a few stores who continue to make it work but they often mix in drop shipping as a way to expand their traditional retail offering or test out new items. As a brand owner, you should consider drop shipping as a means to an end rather than a sustainable revenue source. I recommend only considering drop shipping for strategic partners who will expose your product to a new audience or who have the potential to lead to a larger wholesale relationship. If a website doesn't generate their own traffic by serving a unique niche or attracting potential customers through compelling media, it's unlikely that they will add value to your brand. Instead, they will siphon off your customers through digital advertising and compete with you and your retail partners. After all, they can afford to spend nearly all of their allocated margin on ads since they don't have to invest in inventory.

If you decide to move forward with a drop shipping partner, they should get much lower margins than a traditional wholesale account for all of the reasons previously mentioned. A modest 15% margin is not out of the question for a drop shipping account. The maximum margin I would recommend is 30%, and that should be reserved for a high-quality strategic partner.

You might also want to ensure that any drop shipping partners you on-board can link up to your order management system through an API integration (application programming interface). Otherwise, you'll be stuck uploading or shipping their orders manually and entering tracking information in their system once they're shipped. Most serious drop shippers have pre-built integrations for popular ecommerce platforms like Shopify. These integrations allow for orders to seamlessly flow from their website through yours. The shipments are then arranged at your 3PL and the shipping data is automatically transferred back so the seller can send out the tracking email to their customer. A proper API integration will make your drop shipping partnership virtually effortless.

Pursuing retail placement may not be the best way forward for your brand. With the meteoric rise of ecommerce, you can build a 100 million dollar brand selling entirely direct-to-consumer on a single website. Selling to retail adds vast complexity to your business and there is a lot of value in the simplicity of a direct-to-consumer business. I urge you to thoroughly and consciously weigh the pros and cons of retail before deciding which path you'll take.

CHAPTER 13:

GROWING THE BRAND AND COMPANY

If you have some initial success, you will undoubtedly find yourself looking to grow your brand and your business. Revenue growth results in increased workload, which leaves you needing to hire employees. Once you have employees you need to implement processes and management programs. Your business must constantly evolve in order to sustain growth. This chapter outlines some basics around how to achieve and manage growth in your product business.

13.1: GROWING REVENUE

There are a few fundamental ways to achieve revenue growth in your product business: Sell more of the same product, charge more for the same product while selling a similar number of units, or add another product to your line to sell more total products.

Of these three options, you should strongly consider the first two before you decide on the third. Adding products to a successful brand is called "line extending" and this is pretty unanimously considered to be a bad idea by marketing experts. Line extending weakens your brand and dilutes your message. Having multiple choices on your website turns the buying process into a shopping process. You now require the customer to make decisions before they buy, and that hesitation will often result in the decision not to buy at all. More often than not, line extension will severely damage your conversion rate.

If you choose to extend your line, the new products should be closely related. Different sizes and colors of the same basic product might have less of a negative impact than adding a totally new product to the mix. If you do want to add a totally new product, ensure it compliments your original product and they fit well together. This lineup makes up your brand, and the brand must appeal to the same core customer as your original product.

As you have new product ideas, consider creating a totally new brand and website for each of them. This enables you to grow your company without weakening your brands or diluting your conversion rate. You probably never thought about it, but this is the tactic used by the most successful consumer product companies in the world. Look at Procter and Gamble, for example. They own and operate dozens of discreet brands, most of which are hugely successful. These brands include Gilette, Crest, Herbal Essences, Old Spice, Febreeze, Charmin, Bounty, and many others. Nobody understands the power of branding better than P&G and they choose to operate separate brands rather than diluting existing brands through line extension. They aren't the only ones. 3M operates in a similar way with discreet brands like

Post-It, Scotch, and Command. These are all variations of sticky things that could have easily fit under a single brand, but they chose to brand them independently to avoid the pitfalls of line extension. Once you start to look for it, you'll notice that most successful brands are owned by a parent company that operates a number of different brands. This is no accident, and this strategy should be strongly considered by any product entrepreneur looking to grow their overall business in the most effective way possible.

13.2: GROWING YOUR TEAM

As sales increase, your workload will also increase. You might be able to run the entire business yourself through your first million dollars in sales, but you'll eventually reach the point where you can no longer do it alone. Your first helpers will probably be independent contractors who can take a little of the burden off without drawing a full-time salary. Contractors can plug in to your business and help in a number of areas including bookkeeping, accounting, PR, marketing, photography, web development, graphic design, product development, or nearly anything else you need. They can offer specialized skillsets and knowledge in the amount you need for your business. Most specialized roles will only require a few hours of work per week in a young business, so it would be wasteful to hire full-time positions for these roles.

Contractors are much easier to on-board and manage than traditional employees. You don't have to withhold taxes when you pay a contractor – they are responsible for reporting and paying taxes on their earnings. You can simply pay a contractor by check or credit card.

When you're setting up a contractor in your system, you should request a completed and signed Form W9 from them. This simple form ensures you have the proper information to issue a Form 1099 to your contractors at the end of the year. Form 1099 reports non-employee wages to the government. When you set up the contractor in QuickBooks, simply check the box that says "track payments for 1099" in the setup window. At the end of the year, QuickBooks will enable you to automatically issue Form 1099 to every qualifying contractor with just a few clicks.

It's worth noting that contractors whom you paid less than $600 in a year don't require a Form 1099. Corporations (Inc. or S Corps) are not required to receive a form 1099. Also, contractors you paid by credit card are not required to receive a Form 1099.

The simplicity of hiring, paying, reporting, and managing contractors makes them very appealing for a young product business. You can probably carry on with only contractors for quite some time, but at some point it will make sense to hire your first full time employee. It can be difficult to guess when you'll reach this point or even who or what your first hire will be. In my experience, you know it when you get there.

Your first hires will probably need to be generalists. They will need to perform a lot of different roles and take on a wide array of responsibilities. After all, it's just the two of you running an entire business. As your team grows, your hires will get more specific. Each employee will take a more narrow chunk of the responsibility. As the owner and operator, you should look to hire your weaknesses first. You won't be great at every role within your business, so why not hire for the ones you're worst at? This will strengthen your business and improve your daily life. Most of us hate doing things we're bad at, so why not make someone else do it?

Hiring a full-time employee isn't particularly difficult, but it's much more involved than hiring a contractor. First and foremost, invest in a subscription to QuickBooks Payroll. This add-on to QuickBooks is worth its weight in gold. It will automatically calculate pay and taxes, withhold taxes from paychecks, automate wage withholding payments, and more. It will save you an extraordinary amount of time for the small amount it costs.

Before you hire anyone, you need to set up an unemployment insurance account with your state. This account is legally required and it enables your employees to collect unemployment if they lose their job. You can find the proper resources for setting up an unemployment account on your state's Department of Labor and Employment website.

Most states also require employers to have workers compensation insurance. Qualifying plans are typically bought privately through an insurance company. Most companies that provide business insurance can sell you a qualifying workers compensation plan. The Hartford is one example of a reputable insurance agency that can provide a qualifying workers comp plan for your business. A quick Google search will provide more options if needed.

Once you have QuickBooks Payroll, unemployment insurance, and workers compensation insurance all set up, you're ready to on-board your first hire. This can all be done on the employee's first day. If you're a U.S. employer, you should instruct the new hire to bring either a valid U.S. passport, or a state-issued ID and their social security card. You should inspect this documentation and complete Form I-9 stating that you have done so. Form I-9 can be downloaded and printed from the USCIS.GOV website. Scan this completed form and save a digital copy in your records.

The next step is to have the new employee complete Form W4. You can download and print this form from the IRS.GOV website. You should scan this completed form and save a digital copy in your employee records. You will also need to input the information on this form into QuickBooks Payroll so they know how much tax to withhold from each paycheck.

Once you have the completed W4 you will need to fill out the employee's profile in QuickBooks Payroll. Enter all the relevant employee information the software requests, including pay rate, pay date, hire date, and all other employee data. If you plan on using direct deposit to pay your employees, ask that they bring a voided check on their first day and have them complete a direct deposit consent form prior to setting that up. QuickBooks will walk you through the steps of setting up direct deposit during the employee setup process.

The final step of the hiring process is to report your new hire to the state. This can typically be done by mail or online. To find the proper reporting agency and method to report a new hire in your state, Google search "Report new hire (your state)" and you will get relevant results.

After completing these steps, you will have legally hired your first employee. You're officially on your way to building a successful product empire.

CHAPTER 14:

A CHRONOLOGICAL SUMMARY OF TASKS AND MILESTONES

Starting a product business can seem like a daunting task, and it truly is when viewed in its entirety. The good news is that you only need to take it one step at a time to be successful. This book has outlined nearly every step you'll need to take to become an "overnight success," but it wasn't necessarily written in chronological order. Instead, it was written in a sequence that builds on itself, so a novice entrepreneur would progressively build the knowledge base necessary to understand the upcoming concepts. In this chapter we'll outline the process in chronological order so you always know what to do next.

So many aspiring entrepreneurs start in the wrong place. They rush out and register their business right away, or start building the business's social media account. I've even known some to get branded t-shirts made as their first step in building a product business. All these things seem like fun and they feel like progress, but there is much more important work to be done first. Use these fun milestones as exactly that – milestones. If you do the work and follow the process, you will eventually get your branded t-shirt. These achievements are your reward for hard-won progress. Don't simply skip from milestone to milestone for the dopamine hit or that's all you'll ever get from your modest efforts.

The steps outlined below are intended to be pretty "macro." Use the details in the chapters of this book to break them down into smaller actionable tasks.

Step 1: Have an idea. Come up with an idea you want to pursue or, if you have many, select your favorite.

Step 2: Evaluate your idea. Even great product ideas aren't always winners. You need to evaluate your idea for economic feasibility and technical feasibility. Refer to sections 2.1 and 2.2.

Step 3: Market research. Using the tactics in section 2.4, try to gauge the market potential for your product.

Step 4: Define your target customer. Use the process from section 3.1 to nail down the values, priorities, and needs of your target customer. This will inform the design of the product.

Step 5: Define your product. Create a PRD clearly defining all the important features and specifications of your product. Keep the values of your target customer in mind. See section 7.1 for details.

Step 6: Name your product and develop a logo. See sections 3.3 and 3.4.

Step 7: Determine how you will design and develop your product. Will you do the work yourself or contract it out? Refer to section 7.2.

Step 8: Develop a plan to finance the product development process. You may plan to use your own savings or you might need outside funding. Even if you plan to do the product development work yourself, product development is expensive. You need to plan accordingly. Chapter 5 contains more details on this topic.

Step 9: Prepare your business to accept funding. If you plan to accept outside funding you should register your business and open a corporate bank account at this point. Hire a corporate attorney to help you structure your business entity and generate the necessary documentation to sell shares in your company. Sections 4.1, 4.2 and 5.3 elaborate on these topics. If you don't plan to take outside investment, you might consider registering your company and opening your bank account a little later in the process.

Step 10: Secure funding. If you aren't self-funding, this is where you make your pitch to investors. You'll need to develop a comprehensive business plan for your pitch. Learn more in section 5.3. If you're self-funding it's still a good idea to put together a business plan to ensure your idea is fully baked.

Step 11: Develop your product. Whether you do it yourself or hire it out, you need to turn your idea into a product that is ready for mass production. Refer to Chapter 7 for details on product development and preparation for production.

Step 12: Quote your product. As outlined in sections 7.6-7.9, contact some potential manufacturing partners and get an accurate price quote for your product. You should also calculate your MSRP and make sure the quoted cost of your product still fits within your business plan.

Step 13: Test your prototype and/or pre-production samples thoroughly. Make sure the product does what it's supposed to and can withstand the rigors of regular use. Also ensure you meet all regulatory requirements and get any certifications required to sell your product. This is your last opportunity to make changes. See sections 7.4 and 7.12 for details on product certification and testing.

Step 14: Prepare your product for mass production. This is the time to add SKU numbers and barcodes to packaging, define your inner and master case sizes, apply warning and regulatory labels, and generally take care of all the peripheral details associated with making and selling a product. Sections 8.1-8.4 walk you through this process in detail.

Step 15: Start mass production. Reference sections 7.9-7.14. This process typically takes 60-120 days or more, so you can build out the rest of the business during the production process.

Step 16: Gather assets and build your website. Using your pre-production samples, get some good photos of your product and start building your Shopify website. Chapter 9 walks you through these topics in detail.

Step 17: Figure out warehousing, fulfillment, and shipping. Refer to sections 8.7 and 8.8.

Step 18: Ship your product from the manufacturer to your warehouse. Sections 8.5-8.8 contain all the details on this topic.

Step 19: Go Live. See section 9.8.

Step 20: Drive traffic to your website through marketing. Chapter 10 thoroughly details this process.

Step 21: Refine your website to maximize sales. See Chapter 11.

Step 22: Begin to approach retail stores with your product (if you decide retail is the best path for your product). You can read all about this process in Chapter 12.

Step 23: Grow your business and your team. Refer to Chapter 13.

The chronological steps outlined in this chapter are intended to act as a guide to keep you moving forward. If you get stuck or overwhelmed, just take a look at this list to see where you stand and what comes next. Re-read the recommended sections and execute accordingly.

Building a product business is a marathon, not a sprint. It will take many months or sometimes years to go through this process the first time. The difference between those who succeed and those who fail usually comes down to perseverance. If you hit a wall, do your best to find a solution.

If you can't find a solution, pick a new idea and try again. Nearly everyone, myself included, fails a few times before they find any success. Most of us, myself included again, fail to even get the product to market the first few attempts. Heck, I even failed to finish this book the first time I tried. The defining difference between those who do and those who don't is that the doers don't give up, and that may be the most important takeaway from this entire book.

GLOSSARY OF COMMON INDUSTRY TERMS AND ACRONYMS

3PL: An acronym that stands for "Third Party Logistics." This is a contract warehousing company.

Accrual Accounting: An accounting method where transactions are recorded when they occur rather than when the money actually changes hands. Accrual accounting is required for inventory-based companies.

Affiliate marketing: A marketing tactic that pays media publications a percentage of each sale that they refer.

AOV: An acronym that stands for "Average Order Value." This is the average value of all orders placed on your website, or driven through a particular campaign over a specified period of time.

API: An acronym that stands for "Application Programming Interface." This is a standardized communication format that enables different systems or programs to exchange information.

ASN: An acronym meaning "Advance Ship Notice." This is an EDI term describing the transmission notifying the buyer that a shipment has been initiated.

AVG: An acronym for "Average."

B2C: An acronym for "Business To Consumer." This typically describes a business model where the business is selling to the end customer, rather than to other businesses.

Balance Sheet: A financial statement that reports a company's assets, liabilities, and shareholder equity.

BOM: An acronym for "Bill of Materials." This is a detailed summary of all components and value-adding services required to produce an item that will be re-sold.

Bootstrapping: The act of growing a business using only the profits generated by the business.

Bounce: When someone visits a website but leaves immediately.

Brick-and-Mortar Retail: A term used to describe a retail store with a physical store location

Certificate of Insurance: A certificate issued by an insurance provider stating the coverage levels of the insured and, if necessary, listing other insured parties.

Chargeback: A fee assessed by the buyer of goods intended to cover the cost of logistical mistakes made by the seller and/or shipper.

COGS: An acronym for Cost Of Goods Sold. This is the cost of buying or manufacturing the products that will be resold. This includes all materials, labor, and manufacturing overhead directly associated with the product.

COI: An acronym for "Certificate of Insurance."

Contract manufacturer: A factory that is paid to produce goods for another party.

Conversion Rate: The average percentage of visitors who make a purchase on your website. If you had 1000 visitors this week and 20 of them made a purchase, your conversion rate is 2%.

Cost: The amount paid for an item that will be resold.

Country of Origin: The country in which a product is manufactured.

CPA: Cost Per Acquisition. This is a measurement of the average cost of getting someone to perform a specific "action." With most product based companies the desired "action" is making a purchase. Under these circumstances, this is a measurement of the average cost of acquiring a new customer.

CPC: Cost Per Click. This is a measurement of your average cost to get 1 person to click on your ad.

CPM: Cost Per Thousand Impressions. This is a measurement of the cost to display your ad 1,000 times.

CTC: An acronym that means "Click-Through Conversion." This metric measures conversions after a customer has clicked a digital ad.

D2C: An acronym for "Direct To Customer." This typically describes a business model where the manufacturer is selling directly to the end customer.

DBA: An acronym for "Doing Business As" which is often used to designate a trade name

DC: An acronym that stands for "Distribution Center."

DDP: An incoterms acronym for "Delivered Duty Paid." This means the quoted price includes freight and duties to the customer's final destination. The seller maintains ownership until delivery to the final destination.

Debt Financing: Financing a business by borrowing money that must be repaid.

Design Patent: A type of patent that only covers the ornamental design of a product.

DFM report: An acronym for "Design For Manufacturing" report. This report is intended to identify potential manufacturing issues before mass production tooling is made.

Drayage: A service provided by a tradeshow operator that consists of moving your freight from the loading dock of the convention center to your booth space, and back.

Drop Shipping: A retail relationship where one company sells a product without ever owning or possessing it, and another company ships it directly to the purchaser for a portion of the proceeds from the sale.

Duties: Fees assessed by the federal government for the import of foreign-made goods

EBITDA: An acronym for Earnings Before Interest, Taxes, Depreciation, and Amortization.

EDI: An acronym for "Electronic Data Interchange." This is a standardized communication protocol that enables different computer systems and programs to exchange information.

Equity Financing: A means of financing a business venture by selling shares of the business.

EXW: An incoterms acronym meaning "Ex Works." This means the quoted price includes only the goods made ready to ship. No freight, transportation, or duties are included in the quoted price. The buyer takes ownership of the goods at the point of origin.

Facebook Pixel: A piece of code installed on your website that enables Facebook reporting to track user activity on your website.

FBA: An acronym associated with Amazon.com that stands for "Fulfilled By Amazon."

FBM: An acronym associated with Amazon.com that stands for "Fulfilled By Merchant."

FCL: An acronym that stands for "Full Container Load." This is a freight term used to describe a container shipment that contains only goods belonging to a single party.

FOB: An incoterms acronym meaning "Free On-Board." This means the quoted price of a product includes transportation to a nearby port and loading onto a cargo ship. The seller maintains ownership of the goods until they are loaded on the ship.

Freight Forwarder: A shipping agent that can arrange mass transport of goods across the world.

GA: An acronym that stands for "Google Analytics."

GM%: Gross Margin expressed as a percentage.

GM: An acronym for Gross Margin.

Gross Profit: Total sales minus the cost of goods sold.

Gross Profit: The profit generated by deducting the cost of goods sold from gross revenue, but prior to any other deductions

Gross Revenue: The total amount of sales, before any deductions, over a specific reporting period

GS1: The worldwide provider of UPC product codes (barcodes).

HTS: An acronym for "Harmonized Tariff System." This is the standardized set of numerical codes used to assess duties on products throughout most countries of the world.

Incoterms: A set of pre-defined commercial terms used to define responsibilities and ownership during a commercial transaction.

Influencer marketing: The use of famous or influential individuals to promote your product or brand.

IP Reputation: A rating of how likely emails from your email extension are to be spam.

Keystone: A pricing model that gives a 50% margin to the retailer.

KPI: Key Performance Indicators. These are the metrics you care about most, plan to measure, and will use to determine whether or not your initiatives are successful.

LCL: An acronym that stands for "Less-Than Container Load." This is a freight term used to describe a container shipment that contains goods belonging to multiple parties.

LLC: An common acronym for "Limited Liability Company."

Look-alike audience: A digital advertising audience that is built by targeting customers who share attributes with a selected group of individuals.

Margin: A financial metric used to describe the return on investment, expressed as a percentage and calculated by the formula: Margin = (Price – Cost)/Price

Markup: A financial metric used to describe the return on investment, expressed as a percentage and calculates by the formula: Markup = (Price – Cost)/Cost

Master Case: A case containing multiples units of the same product. This is typically the largest denomination in which a product will be sold.

MOQ: An acronym for "Minimum Order Quantity." This describes the smallest quantity in which a product or raw material can be ordered.

MSRP: A common acronym for Manufacturer's Suggested Retail Price. This is the suggested retail price as determined by the brand who commissions the manufacturing of the product.

Muse: An imaginary persona created to help define, understand, and market to the target customer.

NDA: An acronym for "Non-Disclosure Agreement." This is a common agreement in which one or more parties agrees to protect confidential information that they may acquire during the course of business.

Net Profit: The remaining profit after all expenses have been deducted.

OH: An acronym for "On Hand." This acronym is used in retail reporting to describe the number of available units in physical inventory

OO: An acronym for "On Order." This acronym is used in retail reporting to describe the number of units that have been ordered but not yet received.

Open To Buy: A retail term describing the remaining available budget a retail buyer has to purchase items for resale in their store or category.

Organic social media: This describes the unpaid use of social media.

Permission marketing: Any type of marketing that requires the recipient to opt-in before they begin receiving marketing content.

PI: An acronym for "Pro Forma Invoice." This invoice is sent to the buyer before the goods are produced.

PO: An acronym for "Purchase Order." This is a commercial document issued by a buyer outlining the type, quantity, and agreed price for a specific purchase.

POA: An acronym meaning "Purchase Order Acknowledgement." This is an EDI term describing the transmission notifying the buyer that their purchase order has been received.

PPC: Pay Per Click. This is an acronym used to describe an advertising model where you pay for every click your ad receives.

PR: An acronym for "Public Relations." This typically deals with organic, earned media coverage rather than paid-for coverage.

PRD: An acronym for Product Requirement Document. This document defines the necessary features and specifications of a product, acting as a blueprint for the product development team to design around.

Price: The value at which an inventory item was sold.

Pro Forma Invoice: This is an invoice that is sent to the buyer before the goods are produced.

Profit and Loss Statement: A detailed outline of a company's income and expenses during a specific time period.

Registrar: A company that manages domain registration on behalf of their customers.

ROAS: Return on Ad Spend. A ratio showing the amount of revenue generated per dollar spent on advertising. If you earn $550 by spending $100 on advertising, your ROAS is 5.5:1

ROI: Return on Investment. Similar to ROAS but can apply to the amount spent on anything, not just advertising spend

RTL: An acronym for "Retail."

S Corporation: A taxation election in which the owners of a company elect to receive a salary and be taxed as employees rather than paying self-employment taxes.

Sell-through: The rate at which a product is purchased in a retail store, often measured as a percent of total inventory purchased. Ex. If a retailer purchased 100 units of a given product and they have sold 40 of they, their current sell-through is 40%.

SEM: Search Engine Marketing. The process of getting more traffic or visibility to a website primarily through paid search engine advertising

SEO: Search Engine Optimization. The process of getting popular search engines, like Google, to list you in the top organic results for various search terms.

SERP: An acronym that stands for "Search Engine Results Page."

Silica Packet: A packet containing extremely absorbent media to remove airborne moisture from enclosed areas.

SKU: An acronym for "Stock Keeping Unit."

SLS: An acronym sometimes used on retail sell-through reports meaning "Sales."

SMS: An acronym for "Short Message Service," or text message. This can also stand for "Salesman Sample" in some circumstances.

ST%: Sell-Through Percentage. An acronym used in retail reporting to describe the percentage of units sold of all that were purchased.

TO: An acronym for "Turnover."

TY: An acronym for "This Year."

UPC: An acronym for "Universal Product Code." This is more commonly referred to as a barcode.

Utility Patent: A type of patent intended to protect the functional aspects of a product.

VAR: An acronym for Variance

VTC: An acronym that means "View-Through Conversion." This metric measures conversions after a customer has been shown an ad.

White space: A retail term used to describe unused shelf space. Typically generated after some items are dropped from an assortment, white space presents an opportunity for new products to reach store shelves.

WK: An acronym commonly found on retail sell-through reports meaning "Week."

WOS: An acronym meaning "Weeks Of Supply." This acronym is commonly used in retail reporting to express the ratio between inventory and sales velocity, measured in weeks.

WTD: An acronym for "Week To Date."

YTD: An acronym for "Year To Date."

Made in the USA
Monee, IL
30 October 2024

68970821R00152